HONK, HONK!

Help Nancy Narwhal find her horn.

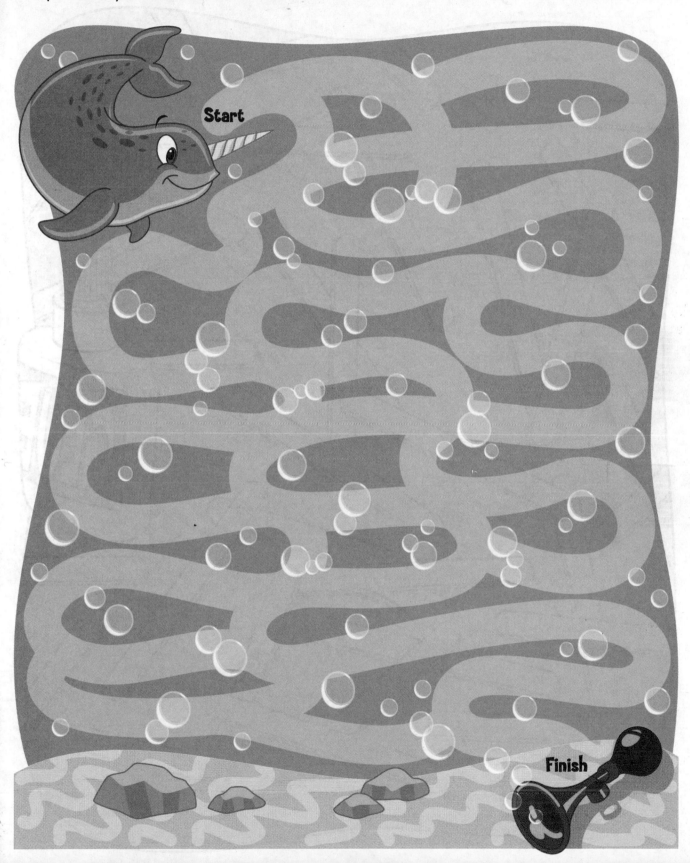

Start

Finish

Mazes

ARTS AND CRAFTS

Follow the maze from start to finish.

Start

Finish

GLUE

GOING IN FOR A LANDING

Help the pelican get to the dock.

Start

Finish

Mazes

OFF TO THE CIRCUS

Help the clown fish make it to the circus.

Finish

Start

Mazes

TIME FOR A NAP

Help the sloth get to his pillow.

Start

Finish

Mazes

IN THE MIDDLE OF THE DESERT

Help the lizard get out of the desert.

Mazes   ©School Zone Publishing Company 06328

PUFFIN AT PLAY

Help the puffin get to his ball.

Start

Finish

©School Zone Publishing Company 06328

Mazes

I LOST MY WHEEL!

Help the caveman find his wheel.

Start

Finish

IN THE ORCHARD

Help the worm get through the apple.

Start

Finish

Mazes

NARWHAL TO NARWHAL

Help the narwhal get to his child.

Start

Finish

TRICERATOPS ON THE GO

Help the triceratops get to his tricycle.

11

Help Rita Raccoon get to the garbage can.

Start

Finish

Mazes

FISHING FOR MY FRIEND

Help the fish find her friend.

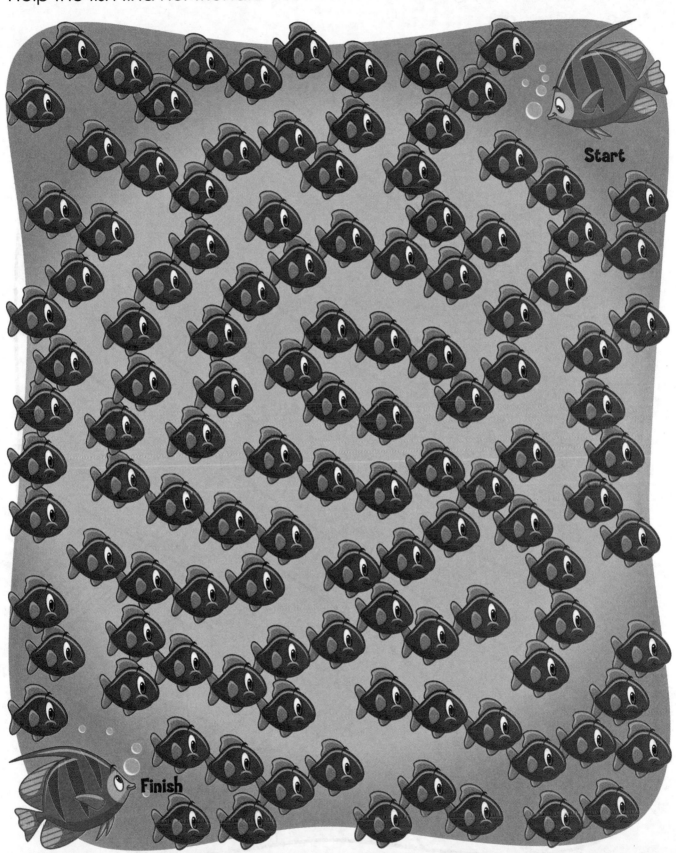

Start

Finish

Mazes

SWINGING BY

Help Monica Monkey get home to her tree house.

Start

Finish

Mazes

©School Zone Publishing Company 06328

SNOWY SKATING

Help the girl get to her friends.

Start

Finish

Mazes

DINNER IS SERVED!

Help the mouse get to his dinner.

Start

Finish

Help Lucky Lemur get to the ice cream.

Start

Finish

Mazes

HANGING AROUND

Help Sammy Snake find his glasses.

Start

Finish

DESERT OASIS

Help Cory Camel get a drink of water.

Start

Finish

Mazes

LITTLE BUDDY

Help the bison get to the mouse.

I FOUND A FINGERPRINT!

Help the detective catch the thief.

Mazes

FOLLOW YOUR NOSE!

Help Buddy the Bloodhound find his toy.

Start

Finish

Mazes

COUNTING YOUR NUTS

Help Sallie Squirrel find her calculator.

Start

Finish

346

Mazes

HOOK, LINE, AND SINKER

Help Felicity Fish get to the worm.

Start

Finish

HOMEBOUND

Help the rabbit get home.

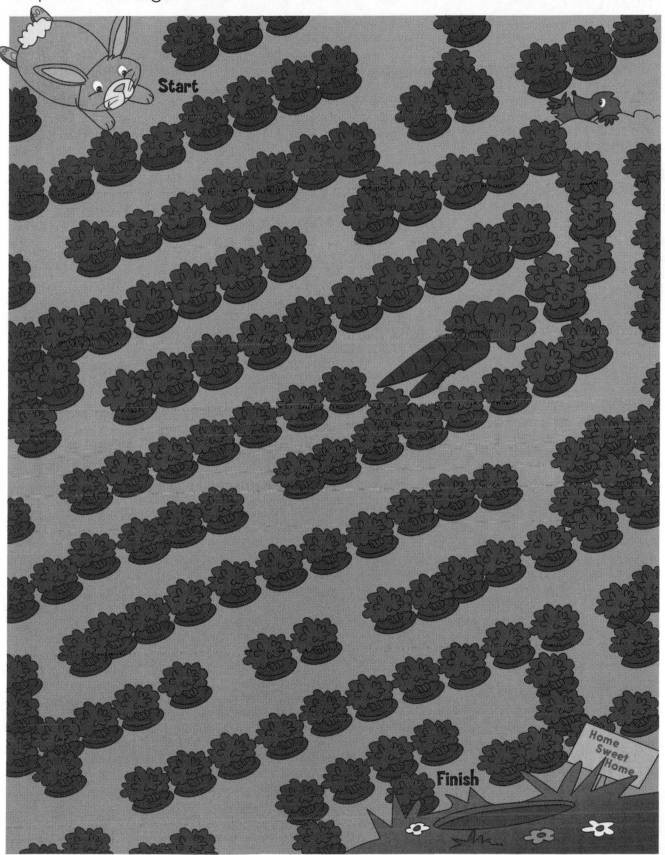

Start

Finish

Home Sweet Home

Mazes

OUT OF THIS WORLD

Help the rocket get to the orange planet.

Start

Finish

NAILS FOR THE HAMMERHEAD SHARK

Help the hammerhead shark get to her nails.

Mazes

FLYING TO THE CASTLE

Help Drew Dragon get to the castle.

Start

Finish

Mazes

©School Zone Publishing Company 06328

UNDERSEA FRIENDS

Help the purple seahorse get to the blue seahorse.

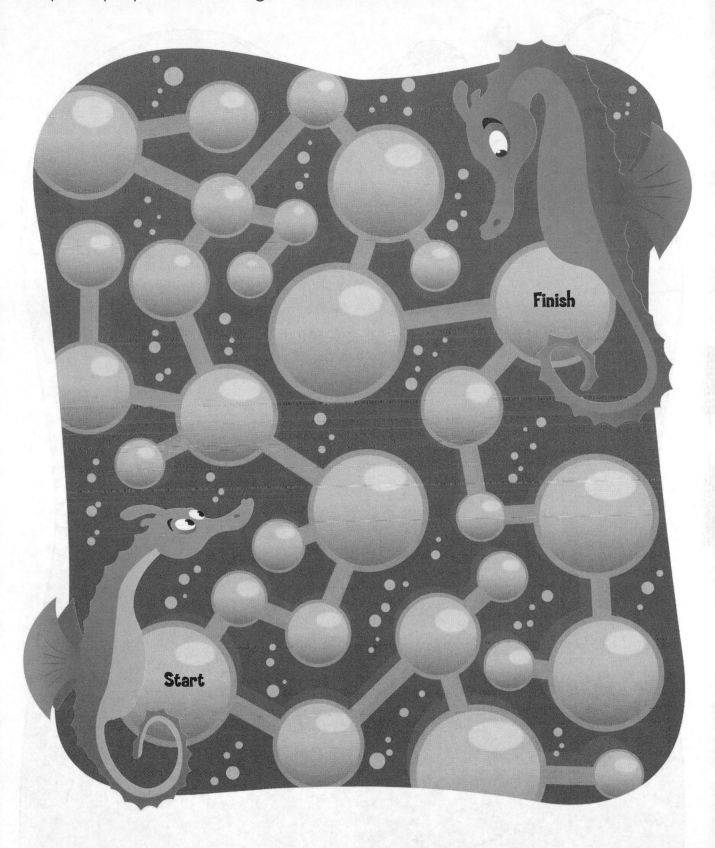

Mazes

CATCHING BUTTERFLIES

Help the girl get to the butterflies.

Start

Finish

TICK TOCK!

Follow the maze from start to finish.

Mazes

Help the alien get the tractor back to Farmer Fred.

MONKEY MAYHEM

Help Monty Monkey get to Simon Squirrel.

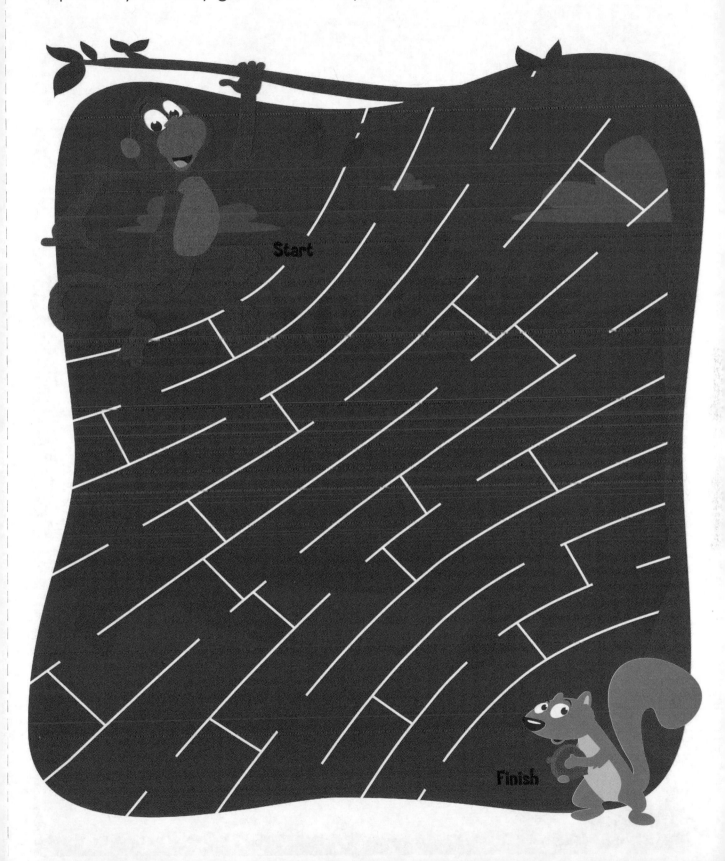

Start

Finish

Mazes

QUEEN'S COURT

Help the king get to the queen.

Finish

Start

Mazes

CALLING ALL PENGUINS!

Help the penguins get to their friend.

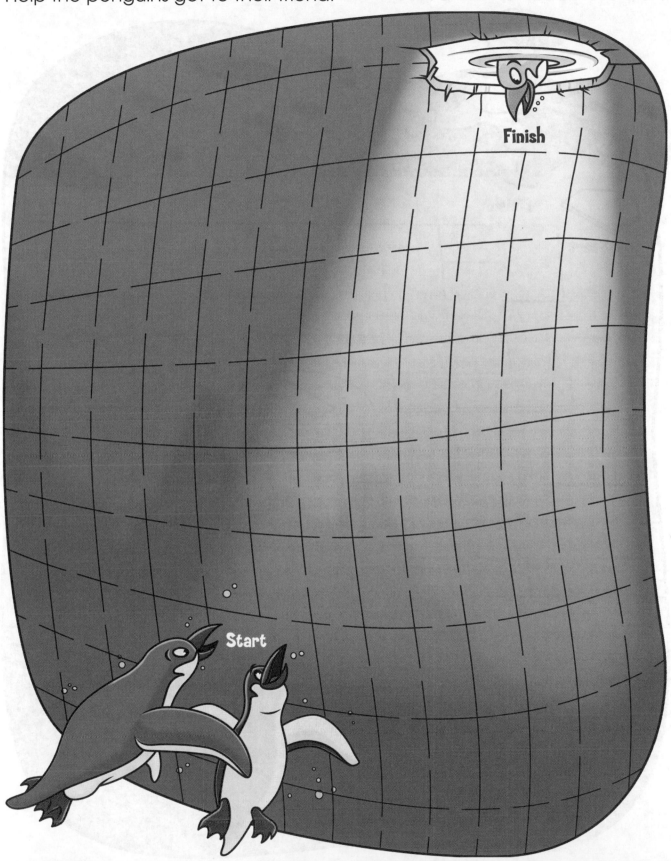

Finish

Start

Mazes

HOME RUN!

Help the batter run the bases.

Finish

Start

Mazes   ©School Zone Publishing Company 06328

CLIMBING AROUND TOWN

Help Kong find where he left his friend.

Finish

Start

Mazes

Help the race car get to the finish line.

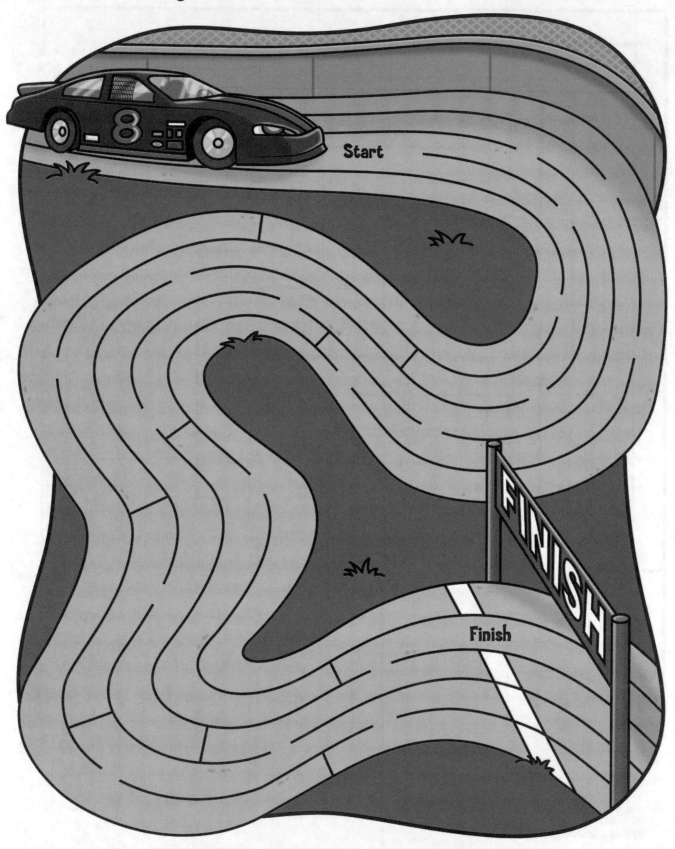

Start

Finish

FINISH

PREHISTORIC FAST FOOD

Help the T. rex get to her dinner.

Start

Finish

T Rek's

Mazes

SOAPBOX DERBY

Help the riders get to the end.

Mazes

STARLIGHT SHOW

Help the firefly get to his performer friend.

Start

Finish

Mazes

LEAKY HOSE

Follow the maze from start to finish.

Start

Finish

THE BIG SPILL

Get to the finish without getting wet!

Mazes

Help Amy and Arthur Ant get to the center of the anthill.

Help the parrot get to her nest.

Mazes

MESSY DESK

Follow the maze from start to finish.

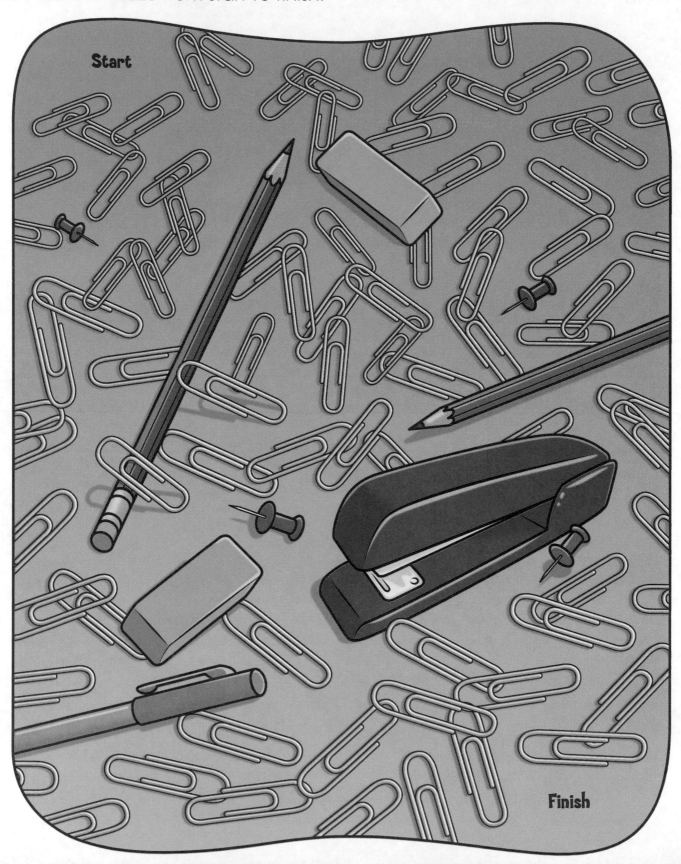

Help the chameleon get to the caterpillar.

Start

Finish

Mazes

ABRAHAM LINCOLN'S HAT

Help Abraham Lincoln get to his hat.

Start

Finish

Mazes

PIGEON PALS

Help Pablo Pigeon get to his friends below.

Start

Finish

Mazes

MAKING A SPLASH

Solve each math problem. Find the first answer on the grid. Draw a line to the second answer. Continue drawing lines to connect the answers in order. When you have finished, a picture will be revealed.

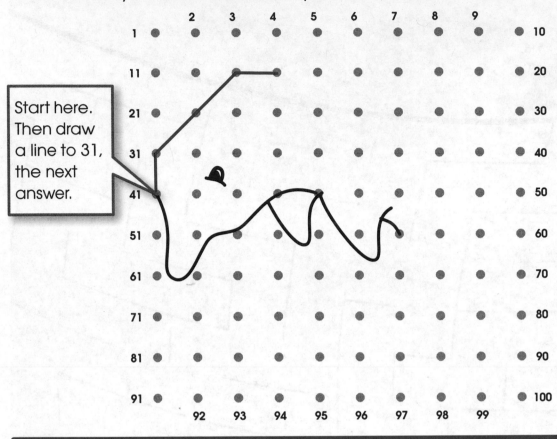

Start here. Then draw a line to 31, the next answer.

Line 1

1. 30 + 11 = ___41___

2. 66 – 35 = ___31___

3. 11 + 11 = ___22___

4. 20 – 7 = ___13___

5. 10 + 4 = ___14___

6. 25 – 10 = _____

7. 6 + 1 = _____

8. 36 – 19 = _____

9. 12 + 15 = _____

10. 77 – 39 = _____

11. 45 + 14 = _____

12. 89 – 20 = _____

13. 66 + 13 = _____

14. 99 – 10 = _____

15. 60 + 40 = _____

16. 100 – 1 = _____

17. 54 + 44 = _____

18. 99 – 2 = _____

19. 44 + 44 = _____

20. 100 – 22 = _____

21. 56 + 12 = _____

22. 87 – 30 = _____

Grid Numbering Example:

	2	3	4	5
1	•	•	•	• •
11 •	12 •	13 •	14 •	15 •
21 •	22 •	23 •	24 •	25 •
31 •	32 •	33 •	34 •	35 •

Math Puzzle Grid   ©School Zone Publishing Company 06328

SCAT CAT!

Color the picture below.

1 = **light blue**	4 = pink	7 = **green**	10 = **black**
2 = **dark blue**	5 = **orange**	8 = **yellow**	11 = gray
3 = **red**	6 = **light orange**	9 = white	

Color-by-Numbers

HOME SWEET HOME

Solve each math problem. Find the first answer on the grid. Draw a line to the second answer. Continue drawing lines to connect the answers in order. When you have finished, a picture will be revealed.

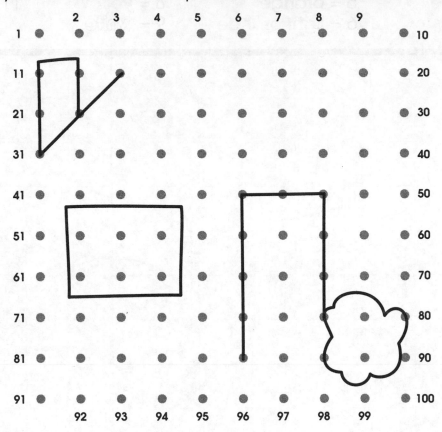

Line 1

1. 35 + 45 = _____
2. 88 - 18 = _____
3. 33 + 27 = _____
4. 75 - 25 = _____
5. 20 + 20 = _____
6. 45 - 6 = _____
7. 13 + 25 = _____
8. 55 - 18 = _____
9. 20 + 16 = _____
10. 65 - 30 = _____
11. 27 + 7 = _____
12. 66 - 33 = _____

13. 16 + 16 = _____
14. 70 - 39 = _____
15. 35 + 6 = _____
16. 61 - 10 = _____
17. 35 + 26 = _____
18. 88 - 17 = _____
19. 44 + 37 = _____
20. 99 - 17 = _____
21. 70 + 13 = _____
22. 95 - 11 = _____
23. 70 + 15 = _____
24. 93 - 7 = _____

25. 72 + 15 = _____
26. 98 - 10 = _____

Line 2

1. 20 + 20 = _____
2. 38 - 9 = _____
3. 11 + 7 = _____
4. 14 - 7 = _____
5. 4 + 2 = _____
6. 11 - 6 = _____
7. 3 + 1 = _____
8. 20 - 7 = _____

Math Puzzle Grid   ©School Zone Publishing Company 06328

MONKEY TROUBLE

Color the picture below.

1 = **light green**   3 = **brown**   5 = **orange**   7 = **purple**
2 = **green**   4 = **light brown**   6 = **red**

Color-by-Numbers

SOMEONE'S CRABBY!

Solve each math problem. Find the first answer on the grid. Draw a line to the second answer. Continue drawing lines to connect the answers in order. When you have finished, a picture will be revealed.

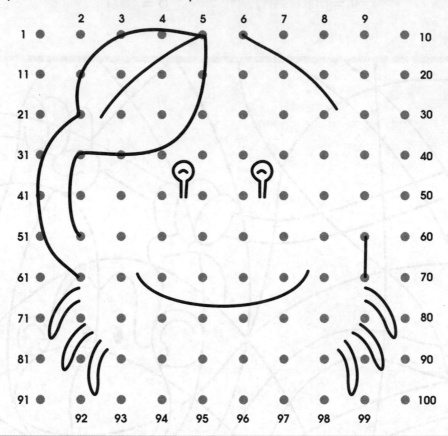

Line 1

1. $43 + 16 =$ _____
2. $74 - 26 =$ _____
3. $34 + 13 =$ _____
4. $53 - 7 =$ _____
5. $32 + 13 =$ _____
6. $88 - 44 =$ _____
7. $27 + 16 =$ _____
8. $78 - 26 =$ _____
9. $39 + 23 =$ _____
10. $88 - 16 =$ _____
11. $44 + 39 =$ _____

12. $93 - 9 =$ _____
13. $43 + 42 =$ _____
14. $92 - 6 =$ _____
15. $48 + 39 =$ _____
16. $96 - 8 =$ _____
17. $71 + 8 =$ _____
18. $79 - 10 =$ _____
19. $50 + 10 =$ _____
20. $75 - 25 =$ _____
21. $27 + 13 =$ _____
22. $43 - 14 =$ _____

23. $8 + 11 =$ _____
24. $44 - 36 =$ _____
25. $4 + 3 =$ _____
26. $24 - 18 =$ _____
27. $13 + 3 =$ _____
28. $47 - 21 =$ _____
29. $22 + 15 =$ _____
30. $84 - 46 =$ _____
31. $25 + 14 =$ _____
32. $66 - 17 =$ _____
33. $46 + 13 =$ _____

Math Puzzle Grid

©School Zone Publishing Company 06328

LOCOMOTION COMMOTION

Color the picture below.

1 = **light yellow**
2 = **yellow**
3 = **orange**
4 = **red**
5 = **pink**
6 = **light blue**
7 = **dark blue**
8 = **green**
9 = **brown**
10 = **light brown**
11 = **black**
12 = **white**

1 / 1	1 / 1	1 / 1	1 / 1	1 / 1	1 / 1	1 / 1	1 / 1	1 / 1	1 / 1	1 / 1	1 / 12	12 / 12	1 / 1	1 / 1
1 / 1	1 / 1	1 / 1	1 / 1	1 / 1	1 / 1	12 / 12	1 / 1	12 / 12	12 / 12	12 / 12	12 / 12	12 / 12	12 / 12	1 / 1
1 / 1	1 / 1	1 / 1	1 / 1	1 / 1	12 / 12	12 / 12	12 / 12	12 / 12	12 / 1	12 / 12	12 / 1	1 / 1	12 / 12	12 / 12
1 / 1	1 / 1	1 / 1	1 / 12	12 / 12	12 / 12	1 / 1	12 / 12	12 / 12	1 / 1	1 / 1	1 / 1	12 / 12	1 / 1	1 / 1
1 / 1	1 / 1	1 / 12	12 / 12	12 / 12	1 / 1	1 / 1	1 / 1	1 / 1	1 / 1	1 / 1	1 / 1	1 / 1	1 / 1	1 / 1
1 / 1	1 / 1	12 / 12	12 / 12	12 / 1	1 / 1	1 / 3	3 / 3	3 / 3	3 / 3	3 / 3	3 / 3	1 / 1	4 / 4	4 / 4
1 / 1	1 / 1	12 / 12	12 / 12	1 / 1	1 / 1	1 / 1	8 / 8	6 / 6	6 / 6	8 / 8	1 / 1	1 / 1	4 / 4	4 / 4
1 / 1	1 / 3	3 / 3	3 / 3	3 / 1	1 / 1	1 / 1	8 / 8	6 / 6	6 / 6	8 / 8	1 / 1	1 / 1	4 / 4	4 / 4
1 / 1	1 / 1	7 / 7	7 / 7	1 / 1	1 / 7	1 / 1	8 / 8	6 / 6	6 / 6	8 / 8	1 / 1	1 / 1	4 / 4	4 / 4
1 / 1	1 / 1	7 / 7	7 / 7	1 / 1	7 / 7	1 / 1	8 / 8	6 / 6	6 / 6	8 / 8	1 / 1	1 / 1	4 / 4	4 / 4
1 / 1	8 / 8	8 / 8	8 / 8	8 / 8	8 / 8	8 / 8	8 / 8	8 / 8	8 / 8	8 / 8	8 / 8	1 / 1	4 / 4	4 / 4
1 / 2	8 / 8	8 / 8	8 / 8	8 / 8	8 / 8	8 / 8	8 / 8	8 / 8	8 / 8	8 / 8	8 / 8	1 / 1	4 / 4	4 / 4
2 / 2	8 / 8	8 / 8	8 / 8	8 / 8	8 / 8	8 / 8	8 / 5	5 / 5	5 / 5	8 / 8	8 / 8	1 / 1	4 / 4	4 / 4
2 / 2	8 / 8	8 / 5	5 / 5	8 / 5	5 / 5	8 / 8	5 / 5	2 / 2	5 / 5	8 / 8	8 / 8	3 / 3	4 / 4	4 / 5
1 / 1	1 / 1	5 / 5	5 / 1	5 / 5	5 / 1	1 / 1	5 / 5	5 / 5	5 / 1	1 / 1	1 / 1	1 / 1	1 / 1	5 / 5
10 / 10	10 / 10	10 / 10	10 / 10	10 / 10	10 / 10	10 / 10	10 / 10	10 / 10	10 / 10	10 / 10	10 / 10	10 / 10	10 / 10	10 / 10
9 / 9	11 / 11	11 / 11	9 / 9	11 / 11	11 / 11	9 / 9	11 / 11	11 / 11	9 / 9	11 / 11	11 / 11	9 / 9	11 / 11	11 / 11

PREHISTORIC PAL

Solve each math problem. Find the first answer on the grid. Draw a line to the second answer. Continue drawing lines to connect the answers in order. When you have finished, a picture will be revealed.

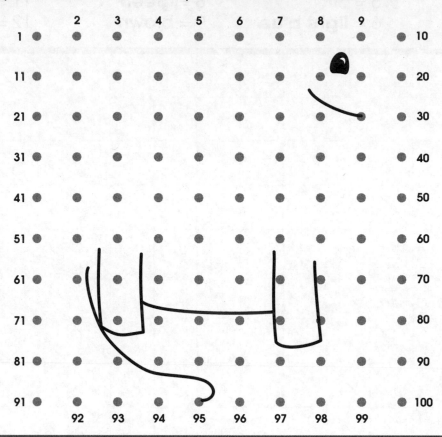

Line 1

1. 33 + 45 = _____
2. 96 - 27 = _____
3. 23 + 36 = _____
4. 66 - 17 = _____
5. 14 + 14 = _____
6. 39 - 10 = _____
7. 17 + 13 = _____
8. 55 - 35 = _____
9. 4 + 5 = _____
10. 16 - 8 = _____

11. 10 + 7 = _____
12. 36 - 9 = _____
13. 39 + 9 = _____
14. 65 - 28 = _____
15. 12 + 14 = _____
16. 50 - 25 = _____
17. 17 + 7 = _____
18. 78 - 55 = _____
19. 20 + 12 = _____
20. 63 - 22 = _____

21. 40 + 11 = _____
22. 77 - 16 = _____
23. 66 + 5 = _____
24. 100 - 18 = _____
25. 80 + 13 = _____
26. 100 - 6 = _____
27. 89 + 6 = _____

56

PURRRRFECT!

Color the picture below.

1 = **yellow**   3 = **pink**   5 = **purple**   7 = **white**
2 = **orange**   4 = **green**   6 = **blue**

Color-by-Numbers

CRUISING AROUND THE TANK

Color the picture below.

1 = **yellow**
2 = **pink**
3 = **red**
4 = **green**
5 = **blue**
6 = **light blue**
7 = **black**
8 = **white**

5/5	5/5	5/5	5/5	5/5	5/5	5/5	5/5	5/5	5/5	5/5	5/5	5/5	5/5	5/5
5/5	5/6	6/6	8/8	5/5	5/5	5/5	5/5	5/5	5/5	5/5	5/4	4/5	5/5	5/5
5/5	6/6	6/6	6/6	5/5	5/5	5/5	5/5	5/5	5/5	5/5	4/4	5/5	5/5	5/5
5/5	6/6	6/6	6/5	5/5	5/5	5/5	5/5	5/5	5/5	5/5	4/4	5/5	5/5	5/5
5/5	5/5	5/5	5/5	5/5	5/5	5/1	1/1	1/1	1/1	5/5	4/4	5/5	5/5	5/5
5/5	5/6	8/6	5/5	5/5	5/1	1/1	1/1	1/1	1/1	5/5	4/4	5/5	5/5	5/5
5/5	6/6	6/5	5/2	2/2	2/2	2/2	2/2	2/2	1/5	5/4	4/4	5/1	1/1	1/5
5/5	5/5	5/2	2/2	2/2	2/2	2/2	2/2	2/2	2/2	4/4	4/5	1/1	1/1	5/5
5/5	5/2	2/8	8/8	2/2	3/3	2/2	2/2	2/2	2/2	2/2	2/2	1/1	1/1	5/5
5/5	2/2	7/7	8/2	2/2	3/3	2/2	2/2	2/2	2/2	2/2	2/2	1/1	1/1	5/5
5/5	2/2	2/2	2/2	2/3	3/2	2/2	2/2	2/2	2/2	2/4	4/5	1/1	1/1	5/5
6/6	5/2	2/2	2/3	3/2	1/1	2/2	2/2	2/2	2/1	4/4	5/5	5/5	1/1	1/5
5/5	5/5	2/2	2/2	2/2	1/1	1/1	2/2	2/1	1/1	1/4	4/4	5/5	5/4	5/5
5/5	5/5	5/5	5/4	5/5	1/1	1/1	5/5	5/5	5/5	4/4	4/4	5/5	4/4	5/5
5/5	5/5	5/5	4/4	5/5	5/5	1/5	5/5	5/5	5/4	4/4	4/5	5/5	5/5	4/4
5/5	5/4	4/4	4/5	5/5	5/5	5/5	5/5	5/5	4/4	4/4	5/5	5/5	5/4	4/4
5/5	4/4	4/4	5/5	5/5	5/5	5/5	5/5	5/5	4/4	4/4	5/5	5/5	4/4	4/5

SPRINGTIME

Solve each math problem. Find the first answer on the grid. Draw a line to the second answer. Continue drawing lines to connect the answers in order. When you have finished, a picture will be revealed.

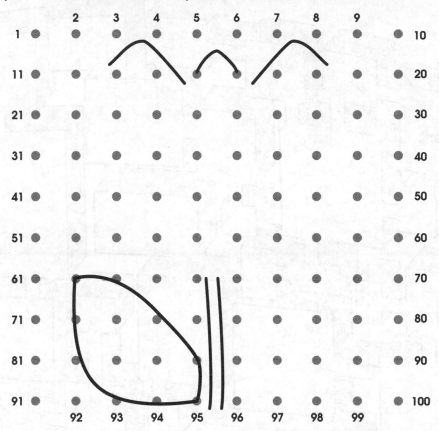

Line 1

1. 8 + 7 = _____

2. 48 - 24 = _____

3. 6 + 7 = _____

4. 8 - 6 = _____

5. 10 + 2 = _____

6. 30 - 8 = _____

7. 17 + 15 = _____

8. 87 - 45 = _____

9. 26 + 27 = _____

10. 87 - 23 = _____

11. 50 + 15 = _____

12. 95 - 29 = _____

13. 40 + 27 = _____

14. 77 - 19 = _____

15. 41 + 8 = _____

16. 75 - 36 = _____

17. 18 + 11 = _____

18. 25 - 6 = _____

19. 4 + 5 = _____

20. 12 + 6 = _____

21. 56 - 29 = _____

22. 9 + 7 = _____

Line 2

1. 82 - 13 = _____

2. 51 + 17 = _____

3. 88 - 11 = _____

4. 73 + 13 = _____

5. 100 - 4 = _____

6. 74 + 23 = _____

7. 99 - 1 = _____

8. 45 + 44 = _____

9. 95 - 16 = _____

10. 55 + 14 = _____

Math Puzzle Grid

Follow the maze from start to finish.

Mazes

TREASURE ISLAND

Help the ship get to the island.

Start

Finish

IT TASTES LIKE DIRT!

Help the anteater find the ant.

Start

Finish

LANDING PAD

Help the helicopter land safely on the landing pad.

Start

Finish

Mazes

OUT OF THE NEST

Help the egg get back to the nest.

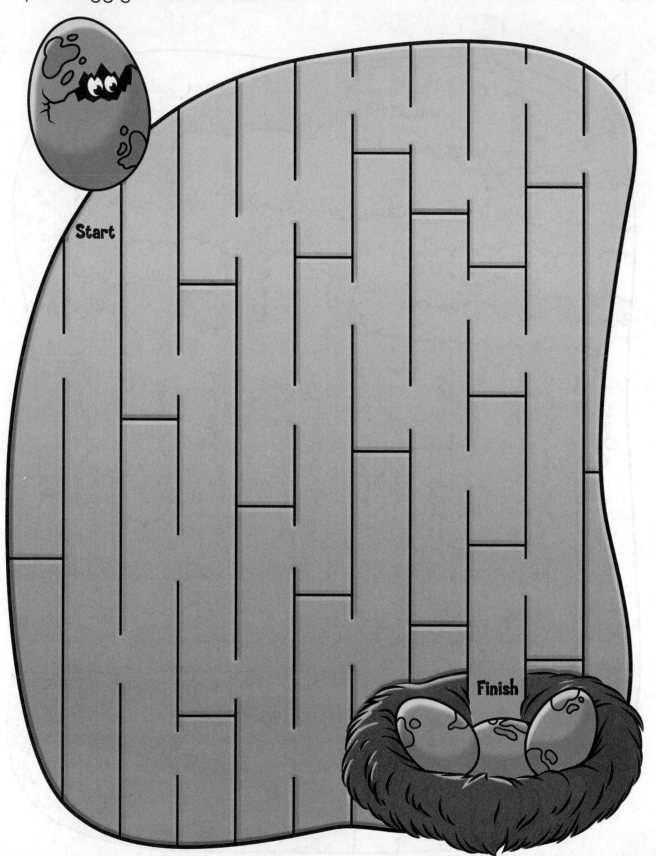

Start

Finish

BARN SWEET BARN

Help the bull get to his home in the barn.

Mazes

BLOWING UP BALLOONS

Follow the maze from start to finish.

NIGHTTIME VISIT

Help Ollie Owl visit Gary Groundhog.

Start

Finish

Mazes

Help George Washington get to the Washington Monument.

ARCTIC AMIGOS

Help Sabrina Seagull get to Wally Walrus.

Start

Finish

Mazes

THE GREAT OUTDOORS

Help the fisherman get to the campfire.

FOREST FRIENDS

Help Hannah Hummingbird get to Marco Moose.

Mazes

Help the bird get to the boy.

Mazes

HIDE AND SEEK

Help Daisy Dog find Buddy Bear.

Mazes

Help the green gecko get to the purple gecko.

SHELL SHINE

Help the turtle get to his wax.

Start

Finish

SNOW DAY

Help Ray Reindeer get to the snowman.

Mazes ©School Zone Publishing Company 06328

BELUGA BUDDIES

Help the beluga at the bottom of the page get to his friend.

Finish

Start

Mazes

SWEET, SWEET HONEY!

Help the bee get to the honey.

Mazes

IN THE BACKYARD

Help the dog get back to his house.

Start

Finish

Mazes

Help the rabbit get to the carrots.

Mazes

PELICAN BAY

Help the pelican get to her perch.

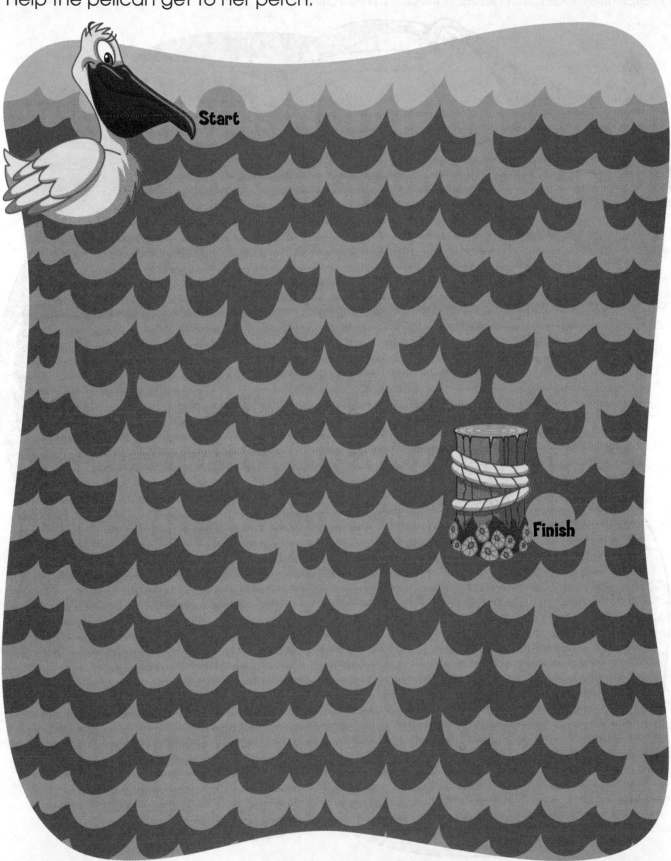

Mazes

Help the toucan move through the rainforest.

Start

Finish

A LEMUR AND HIS FRIEND

Help the lemur get to the bird.

Mazes

Help Finley Fox get across the bridges.

Start

Finish

BEAUTIFUL BUTTERFLY

Help the butterfly get to the flowers.

©School Zone Publishing Company 06328

Mazes

DROP-OFF

Follow the maze from start to finish.

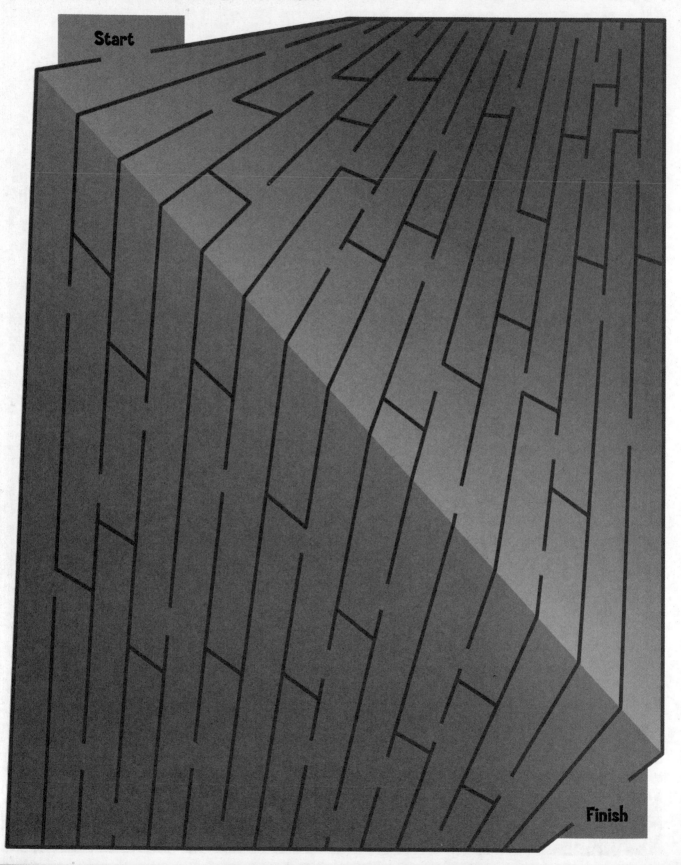

Start

Finish

Mazes

BUILDING A HOME

Help Bertha Beaver get to her home.

MAISY'S HAMSTER MAZE

Help the hamster get to her bed.

Mazes   ©School Zone Publishing Company 06328

SUIT UP!

Help Percy Penguin get to his suit.

Start

Finish

Mazes

Follow the maze from start to finish.

Start

Finish

Mazes

AT YOUR SERVICE

Help the waiter get to the table.

Mazes

Help Ron Raccoon get to Felix Flamingo.

Start

Finish

DINOSAUR FALLS

Follow the maze from start to finish.

Start

Finish

Mazes

CANOE TRIP

Help the girl get to the dock.

Start

Finish

Mazes

Help the lion get to his cub.

Start

Finish

©School Zone Publishing Company 06328

Mazes

CITY TRAFFIC

Help the taxi get to the hotel.

GLORIOUS GIFTS

Help Rex Rhinoceros get to each of his three gifts.

Start

Finish

Finish

Finish

Mazes

FLYING OUT FOR THE NIGHT

Help the bat get out of the cave.

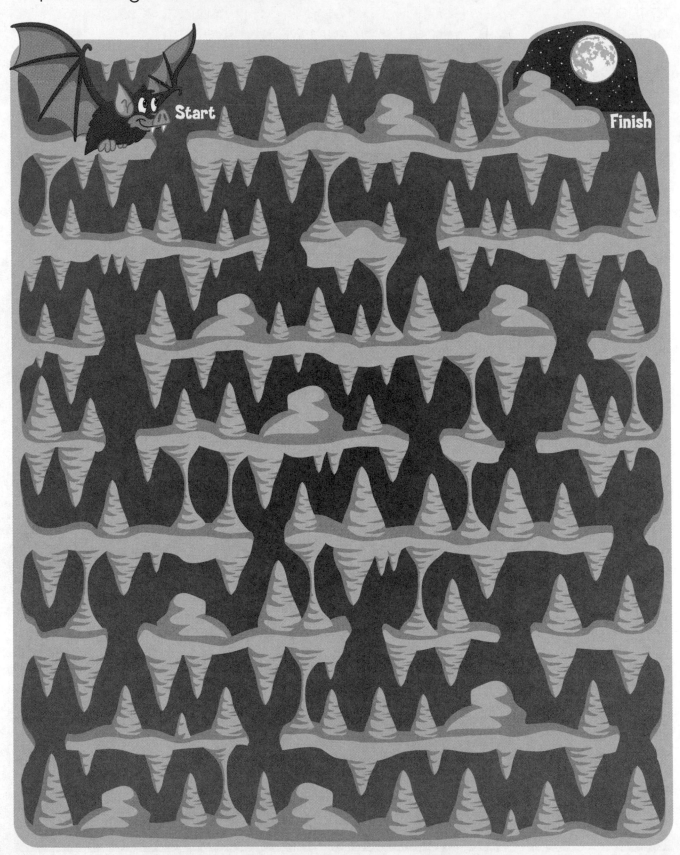

CRUISING ALONG

Solve each math problem. Find the first answer on the grid. Draw a line to the second answer. Continue drawing lines to connect the answers in order. When you have finished, a picture will be revealed.

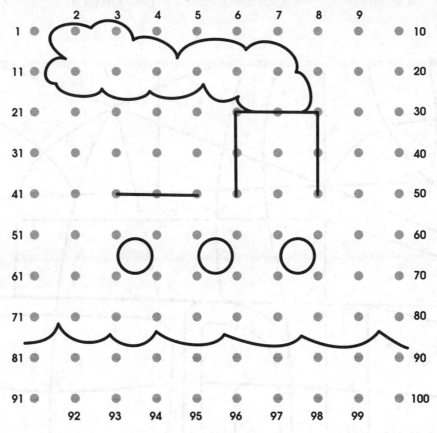

Line 1

1. 37 + 13 = _____
2. 63 - 14 = _____
3. 35 + 13 = _____
4. 66 - 19 = _____
5. 26 + 20 = _____
6. 90 - 45 = _____
7. 18 + 17 = _____
8. 44 - 19 = _____
9. 13 + 11 = _____
10. 50 - 27 = _____

11. 26 + 7 = _____
12. 88 - 45 = _____
13. 22 + 20 = _____
14. 75 - 34 = _____
15. 33 + 18 = _____
16. 88 - 27 = _____
17. 50 + 22 = _____
18. 100 - 17 = _____
19. 42 + 42 = _____
20. 98 - 13 = _____

21. 72 + 14 = _____
22. 99 - 12 = _____
23. 45 + 43 = _____
24. 89 - 10 = _____
25. 46 + 24 = _____
26. 90 - 30 = _____
27. 25 + 25 = _____

Math Puzzle Grid

TRAVELING TRUCK

Color the picture below.

1 = **purple** 3 = **black** 5 = **green** 7 = **red** 9 = **white**
2 = **yellow** 4 = **gray** 6 = **orange** 8 = **blue**

SOMETHING IS FISHY!

Solve each math problem. Find the first answer on the grid. Draw a line to the second answer. Continue drawing lines to connect the answers in order. When you have finished, a picture will be revealed.

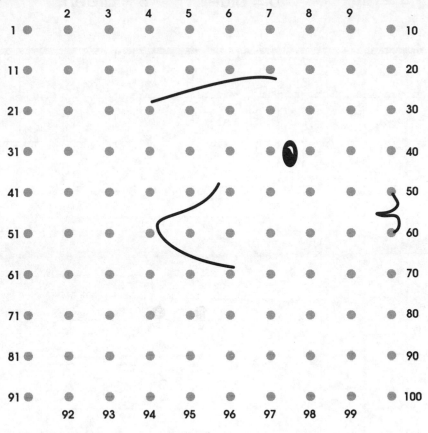

Line 1

1. 25 + 25 = _____

2. 48 - 9 = _____

3. 14 + 14 = _____

4. 36 - 19 = _____

5. 3 + 3 = _____

6. 10 - 5 = _____

7. 3 + 1 = _____

8. 10 - 7 = _____

9. 10 + 4 = _____

10. 50 - 26 = _____

11. 23 + 20 = _____

12. 36 - 14 = _____

13. 0 + 1 = _____

14. 18 - 7 = _____

15. 14 + 7 = _____

16. 63 - 32 = _____

17. 40 + 12 = _____

18. 99 - 28 = _____

19. 45 + 36 = _____

20. 75 + 16 = _____

21. 99 - 27 = _____

22. 45 + 18 = _____

23. 88 - 14 = _____

24. 65 + 20 = _____

25. 93 - 7 = _____

26. 77 + 10 = _____

27. 99 - 11 = _____

28. 44 + 35 = _____

29. 70 - 10 = _____

Math Puzzle Grid

VISITING EARTH

Color the picture below.

1 = **yellow** 3 = **red** 5 = **purple** 7 = **dark blue** 9 = **white**
2 = **orange** 4 = **pink** 6 = **blue** 8 = **green**

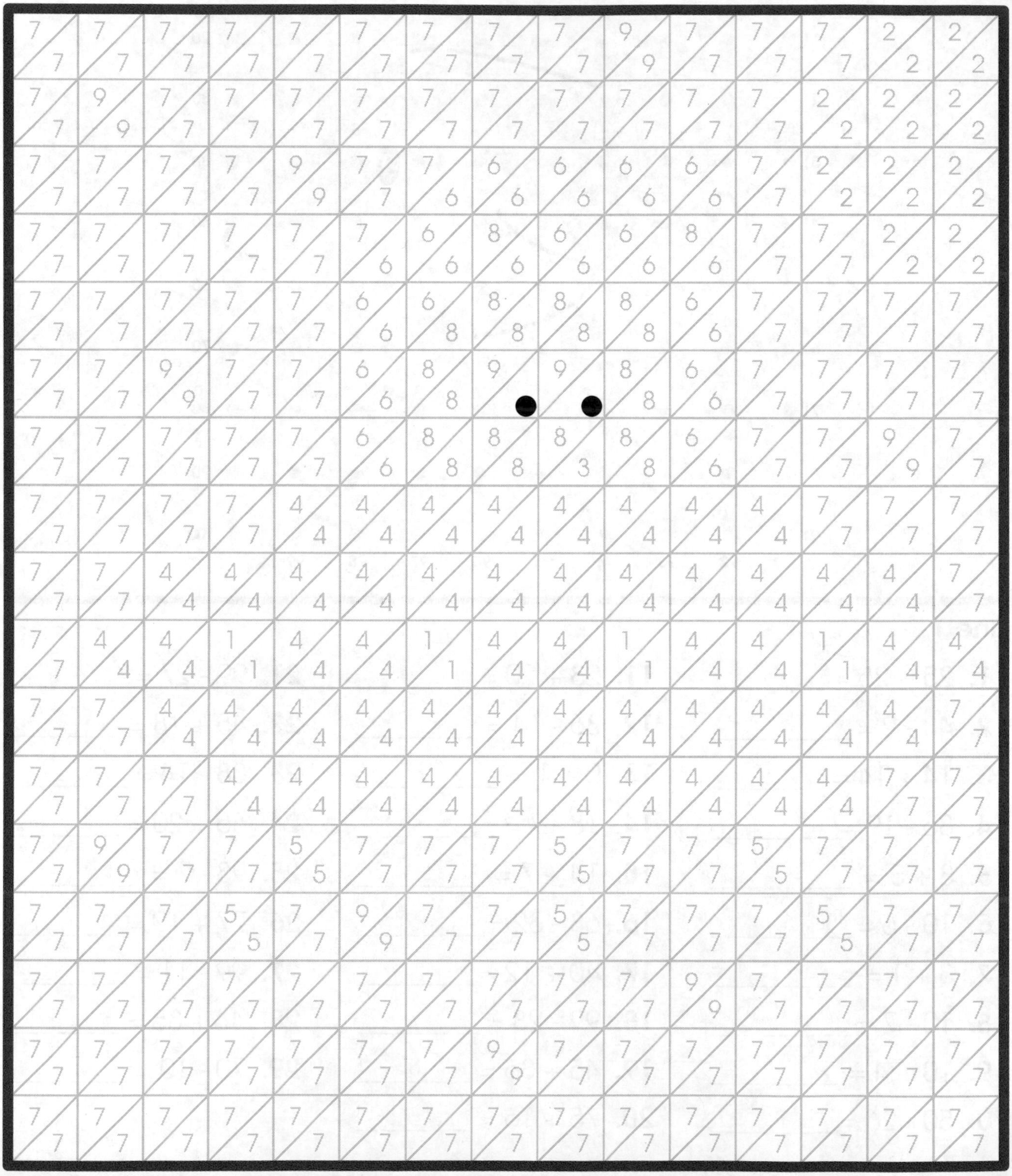

A HAPPY HOPPER

Solve each math problem. Find the first answer on the grid. Draw a line to the second answer. Continue drawing lines to connect the answers in order. When you have finished, a picture will be revealed.

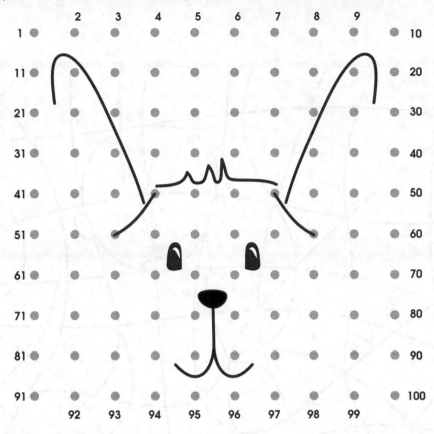

Line 1

1. 83 - 39 = _____

2. 30 + 4 = _____

3. 28 - 15 = _____

4. 8 - 6 = _____

5. 0 + 1 = _____

6. 22 - 11 = _____

7. 17 + 4 = _____

8. 21 + 21 = _____

9. 78 - 25 = _____

10. 58 + 4 = _____

11. 89 - 17 = _____

12. 40 + 42 = _____

13. 100 - 7 = _____

14. 99 - 5 = _____

15. 72 + 23 = _____

16. 99 - 3 = _____

17. 45 + 52 = _____

18. 99 - 1 = _____

19. 66 + 23 = _____

20. 89 - 10 = _____

21. 57 + 12 = _____

22. 77 - 19 = _____

23. 39 + 10 = _____

24. 60 - 30 = _____

25. 18 + 2 = _____

26. 5 + 5 = _____

27. 19 - 10 = _____

28. 15 + 3 = _____

29. 58 - 21 = _____

30. 33 + 14 = _____

103

Math Puzzle Grid

Color the picture below.

1 = **yellow**   3 = **green**   5 = **purple**   7 = gray
2 = **blue**   4 = **orange**   6 = **red**   8 = **brown**

Color-by-Numbers   ©School Zone Publishing Company 06328

NIGHTTIME FRIEND

Solve each math problem. Find the first answer on the grid. Draw a line to the second answer. Continue drawing lines to connect the answers in order. When you have finished, a picture will be revealed.

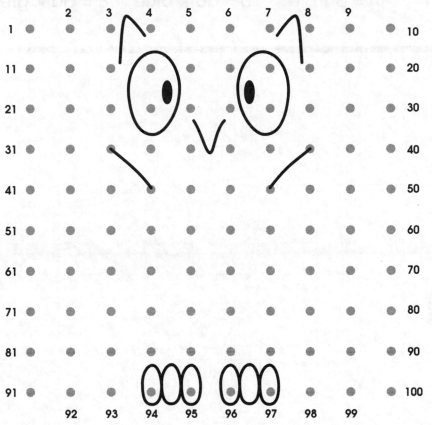

Line 1

1. 2 + 2 = _____

2. 17 - 4 = _____

3. 13 + 10 = _____

4. 36 - 3 = _____

5. 39 + 3 = _____

6. 50 + 2 = _____

7. 70 - 8 = _____

8. 50 + 22 = _____

9. 100 - 17 = _____

10. 90 + 4 = _____

11. 100 - 5 = _____

12. 80 + 16 = _____

13. 50 + 47 = _____

14. 44 + 44 = _____

15. 85 - 6 = _____

16. 60 + 9 = _____

17. 49 + 10 = _____

18. 50 - 1 = _____

19. 30 + 8 = _____

20. 19 + 9 = _____

21. 9 + 9 = _____

22. 4 + 3 = _____

23. 3 + 3 = _____

24. 6 - 1 = _____

25. 4 - 0 = _____

Line 2

1. 22 + 22 = _____

2. 50 + 4 = _____

3. 50 - 5 = _____

4. 30 + 25 = _____

5. 66 - 20 = _____

6. 49 + 8 = _____

7. 70 - 23 = _____

©School Zone Publishing Company 06328

Math Puzzle Grid

A FLUTTER OF WINGS

Color the picture below.

1 = **light yellow**   3 = pink   5 = **blue**   7 = **green**   9 = white
2 = **orange**   4 = **purple**   6 = **dark blue**   8 = **dark green**

Solve each math problem. Find the first answer on the grid. Draw a line to the second answer. Continue drawing lines to connect the answers in order. When you have finished, a picture will be revealed.

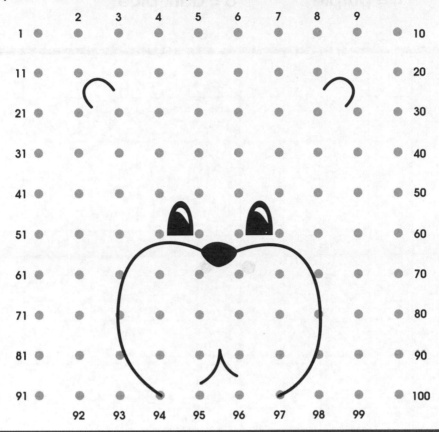

Line 1

1. $90 + 8 =$ _____
2. $100 - 11 =$ _____
3. $65 + 14 =$ _____
4. $75 - 6 =$ _____
5. $30 + 29 =$ _____
6. $39 + 10 =$ _____
7. $40 - 1 =$ _____
8. $15 + 15 =$ _____
9. $25 - 5 =$ _____
10. $4 + 5 =$ _____
11. $12 - 4 =$ _____

12. $10 + 7 =$ _____
13. $30 - 3 =$ _____
14. $13 + 13 =$ _____
15. $31 - 6 =$ _____
16. $16 + 8 =$ _____
17. $23 - 9 =$ _____
18. $1 + 2 =$ _____
19. $3 - 1 =$ _____
20. $10 + 1 =$ _____
21. $25 - 4 =$ _____
22. $16 + 16 =$ _____

23. $45 - 3 =$ _____
24. $40 + 12 =$ _____
25. $70 - 8 =$ _____
26. $69 + 3 =$ _____
27. $96 - 14 =$ _____
28. $70 + 23 =$ _____
29. $100 - 6 =$ _____
30. $53 + 42 =$ _____
31. $99 - 3 =$ _____
32. $74 + 23 =$ _____
33. $99 - 1 =$ _____

Math Puzzle Grid

IN THE ARCTIC CIRCLE

Color the picture below.

1 = **orange**   3 = **light purple**   5 = **blue**   7 = **white** 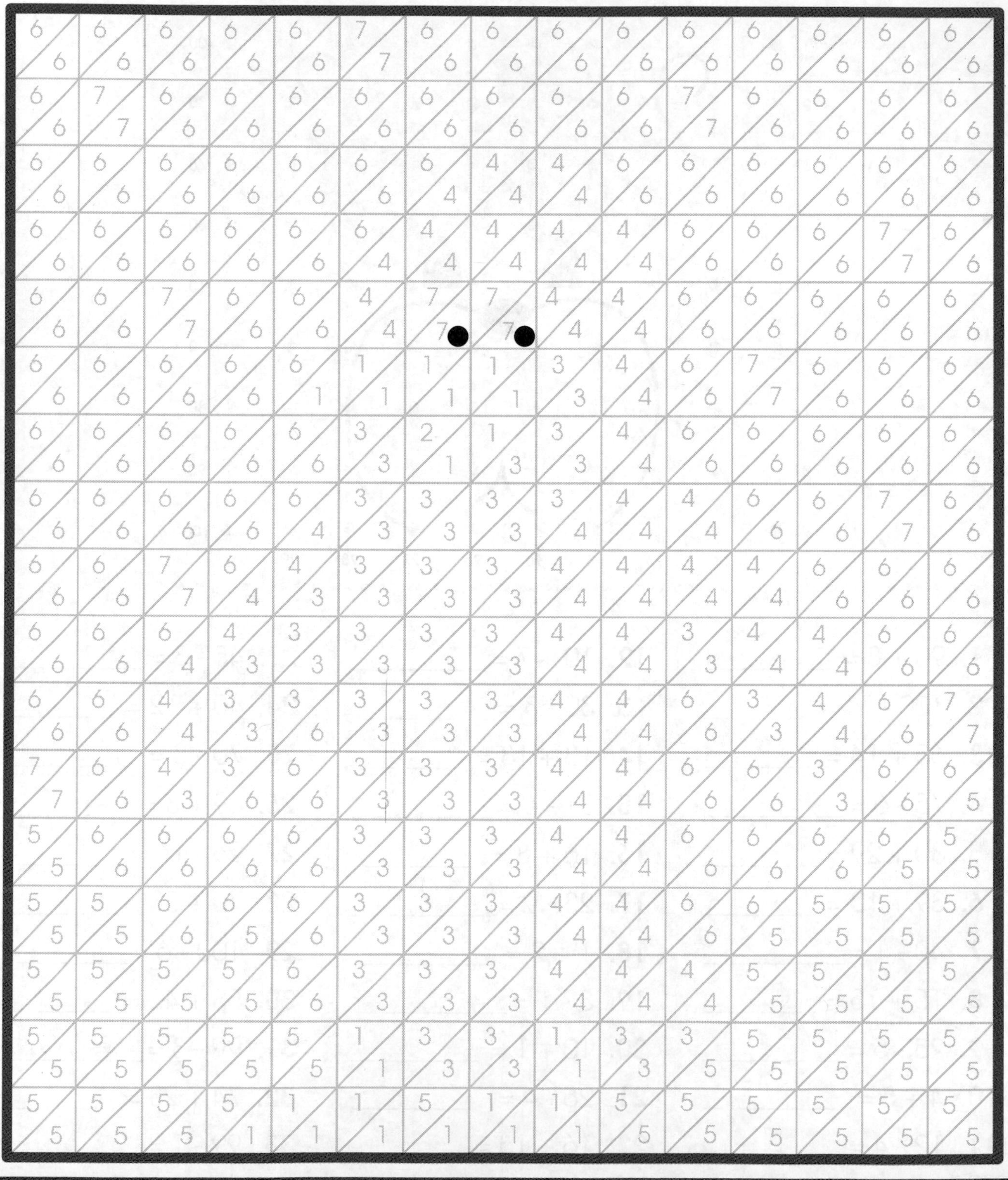
2 = **red**   4 = **purple**   6 = **dark blue**

Color-by-Numbers   ©School Zone Publishing Company 06328

HAPPY PIG

Help Penny Pig get to her friend.

Start

Finish

Mazes

Follow the maze from start to finish.

Mazes

©School Zone Publishing Company 06328

BENJAMIN FRANKLIN'S EXPERIMENT

Help Benjamin Franklin get to the key.

Mazes

GOAL TIME

Help Peter Porcupine get to his soccer ball.

Start

Finish

Mazes

PINK PATH

Follow the maze from start to finish.

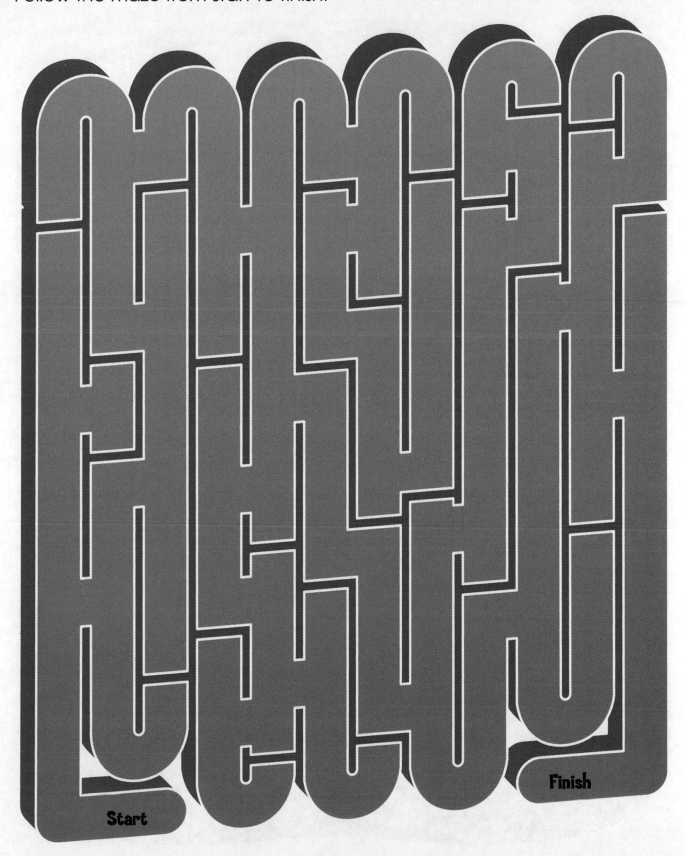

Start

Finish

Mazes

YUM... SEAWEED!

Help the turtle get to a snack.

Start

Finish

Mazes

KEEP PADDLING!

Help the girl paddle down the river. Watch out for the rocks!

Mazes

TRAFFIC JAM

Help the police officer get to the traffic jam.

Mazes

©School Zone Publishing Company 06328

LEPRECHAUN HOP

Follow the maze from start to finish.

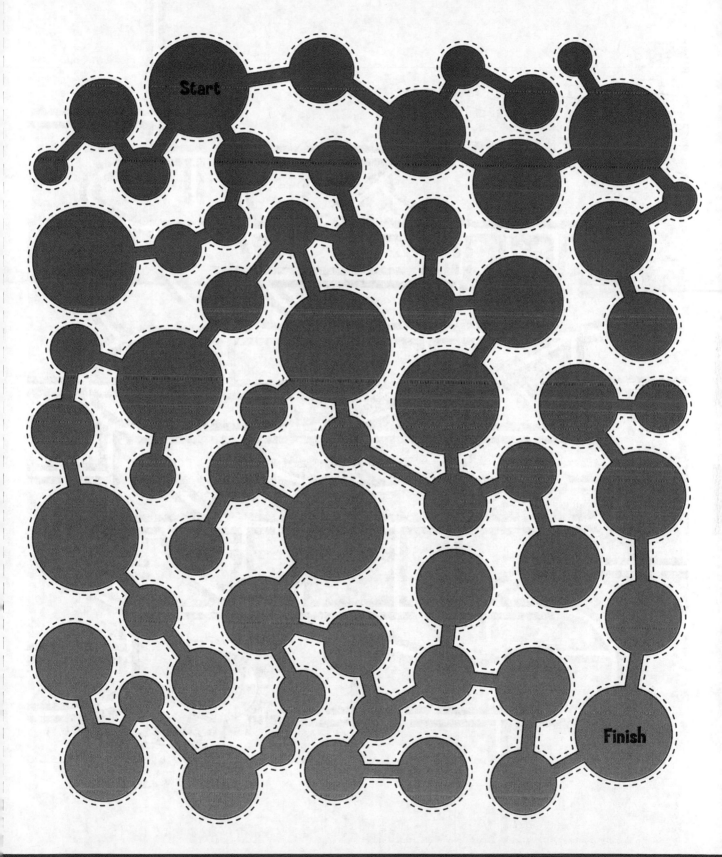

Mazes

FAST TRACK

Help the train reach the traveler.

Mazes

DOLL FACTORY

Help the dolls get to their friends.

Start

Finish

Mazes

LATE DATE

Help the late man get to the girl fast!

Start

Finish

Mazes

SCORE A GOAL!

Follow the maze from start to finish.

Mazes

WARM WATERS

Help the starfish get to the stingray.

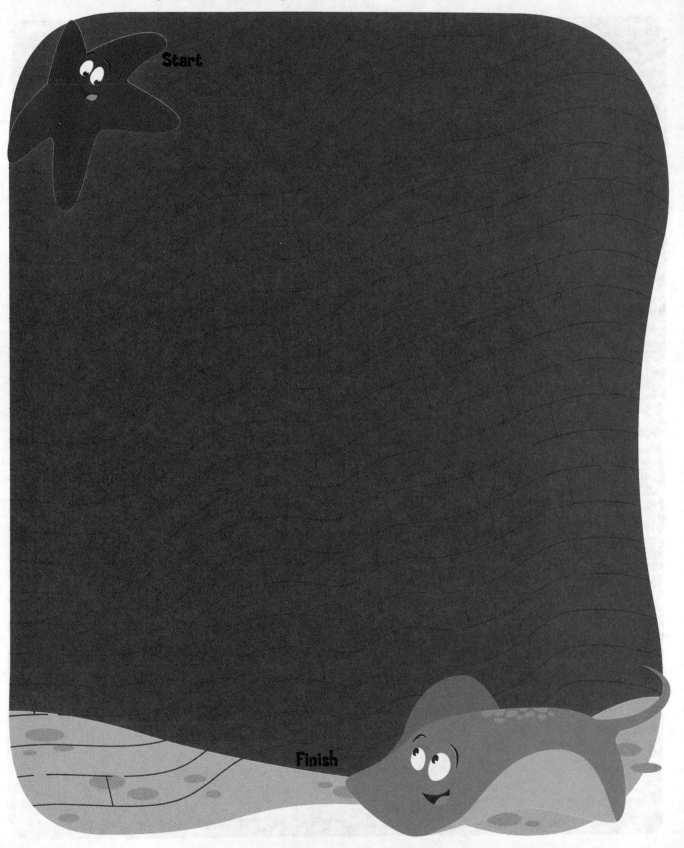

Start

Finish

Mazes

©School Zone Publishing Company 06328

JUST DUCKY!

Help David Duck get to Patty Platypus.

Start

Finish

Mazes

Follow the maze from start to finish.

Start

Finish

MR. FOX LOOKING FOR HIS SOCKS

Help Mr. Fox get to his socks.

Mazes

SLEEPYHEAD

Help the boy shut off his alarm clock.

Mazes

PAR FOR THE COURSE

Help the golfer putt the golf ball into the hole.

Mazes

Follow the maze from start to finish.

Start

Finish

COLOSSAL FOSSIL

Help the children get to the dinosaur exhibit.

Mazes

PREHISTORIC PALS

Help Patty Pterodactyl get to her dinosaur friend.

Mazes

RUNNING IN PLACE

Help the hamster get to the exercise wheel.

Start

Finish

Mazes

WALKING ON STILTS

Follow the maze from start to finish.

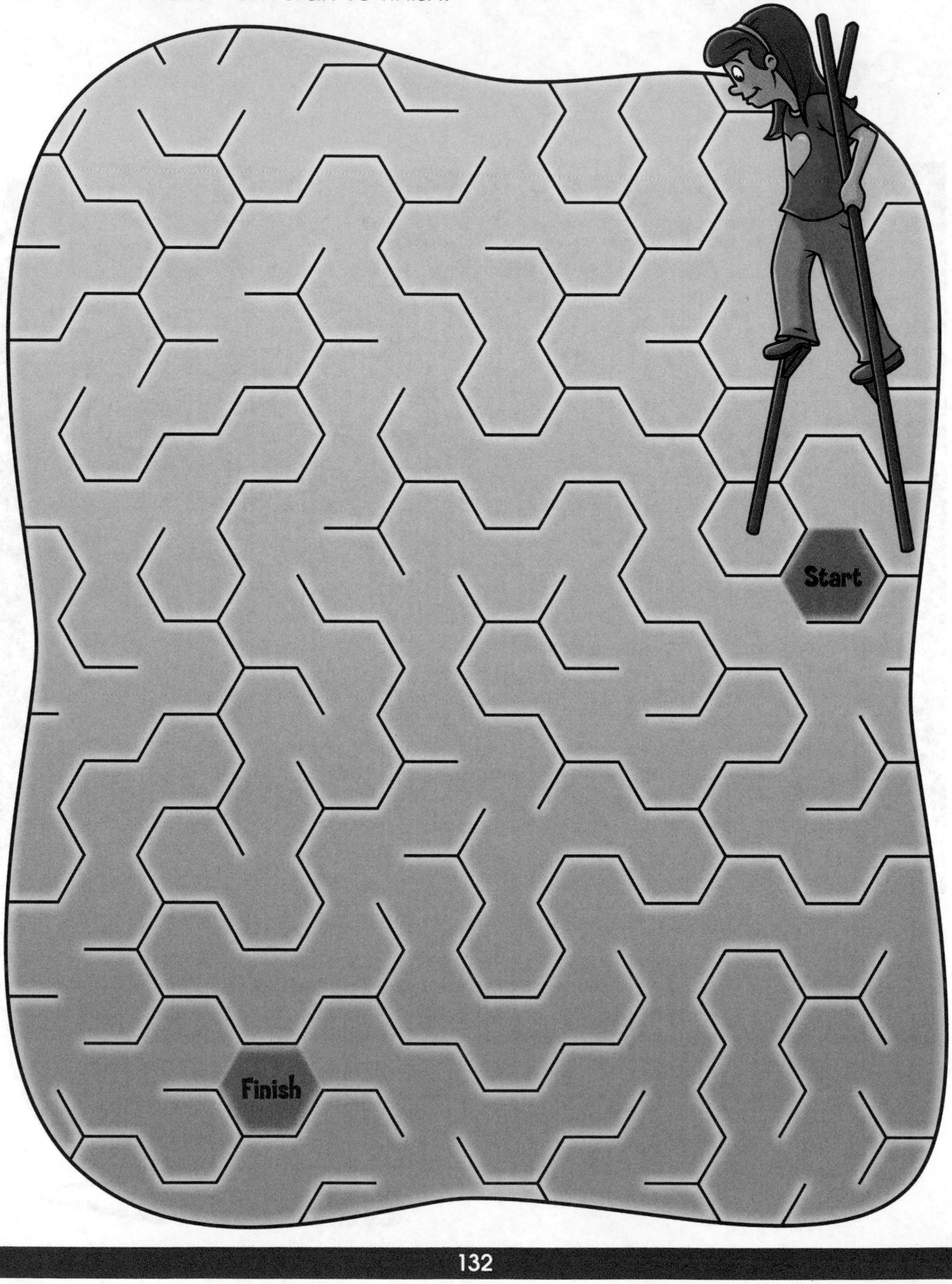

Start

Finish

RUNAWAY CAR

Help the man get to his car.

Start

Finish

Mazes

UNDERWATER PALS

Help the clam get to the lobster.

Start

Finish

Mazes

Follow the maze from start to finish.

©School Zone Publishing Company 06328

Mazes

Help Roxy Robin get to her birdhouse.

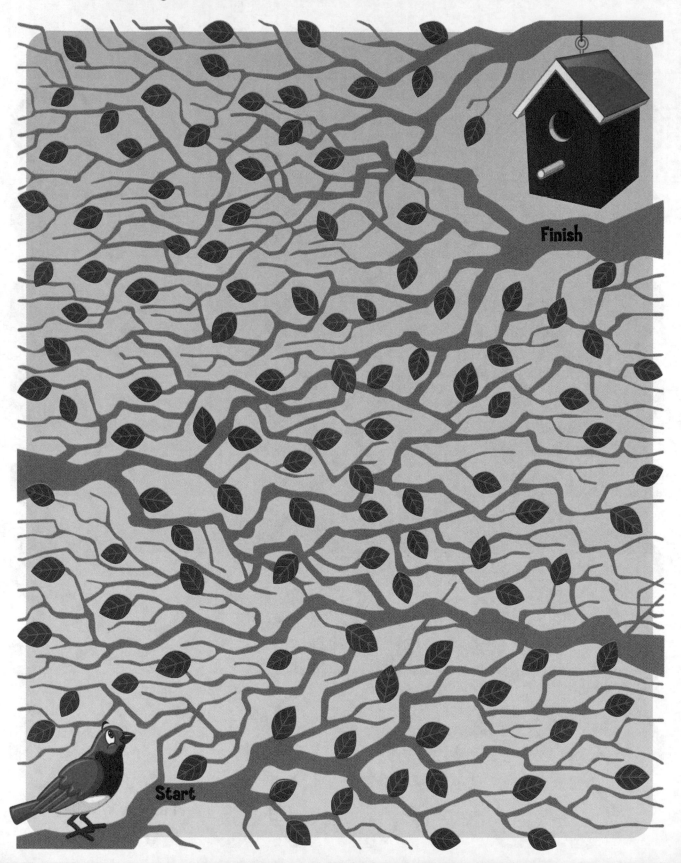

Finish

Start

DANCING RIBBONS

Help the dancer find her slippers.

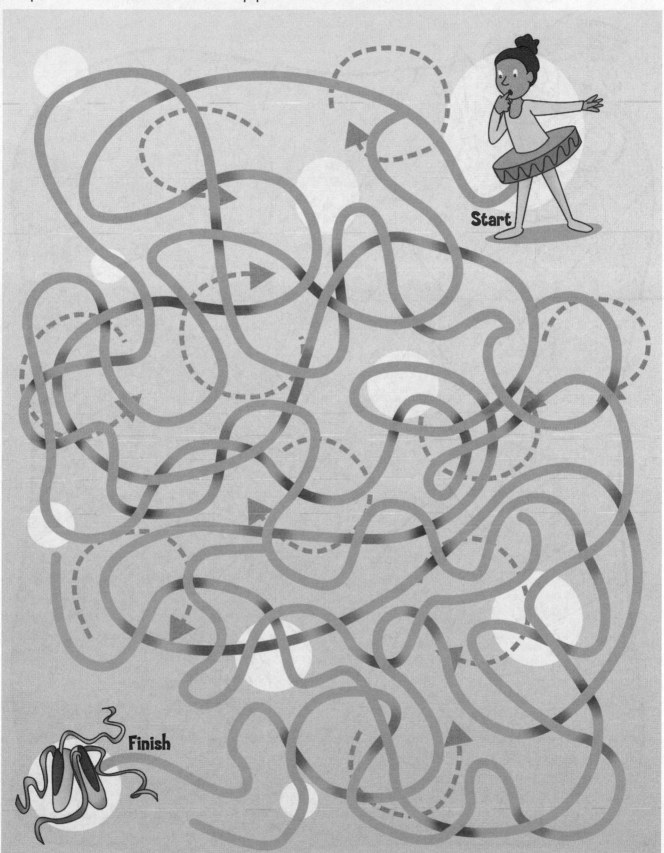

Start

Finish

©School Zone Publishing Company 06328

Mazes

Help the knight get to the dragon.

Start

Finish

BEACH BUM

Help the boy get to the water.

Start

Finish

Mazes

DINNER FOR ONE!

Help the spider get to the center of the web.

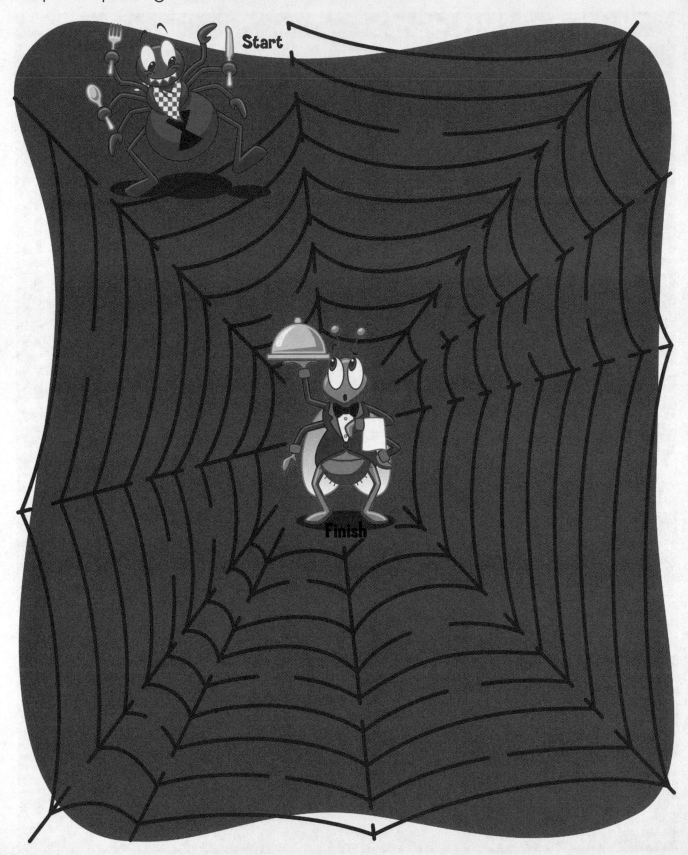

STARBURST

Follow the maze from start to finish.

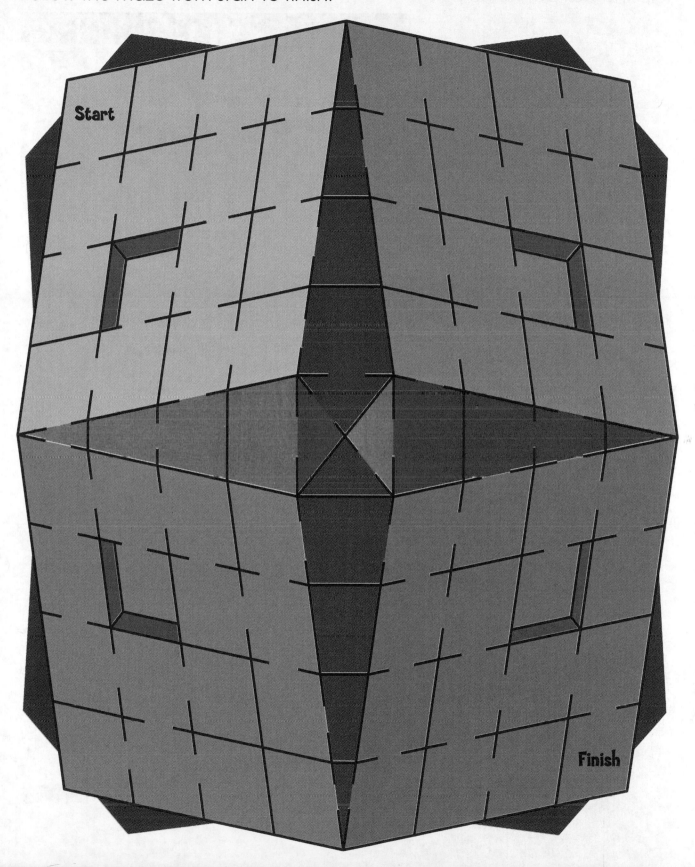

Start

Finish

©School Zone Publishing Company 06328

Mazes

STRIKE!

Help the ball get to the pins.

Finish

Start

DAILY DELIVERY

Help the delivery truck get to the city.

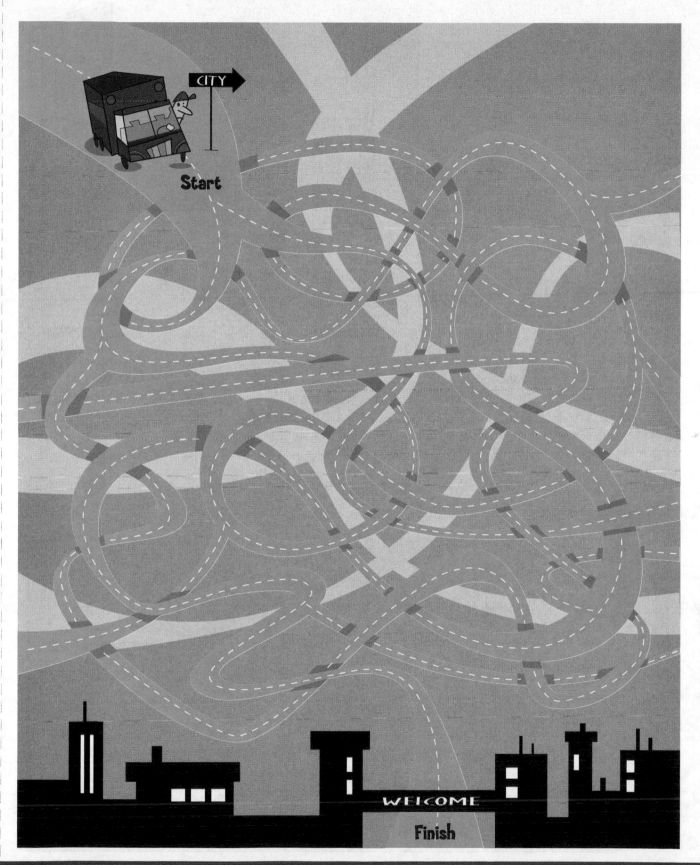

Mazes

DOWN THE LADDER

Help the rabbit climb up and down the ladders to get to the exit.

Mazes

©School Zone Publishing Company 06328

TOOLS OF THE TRADE

Help the construction worker get to his tools.

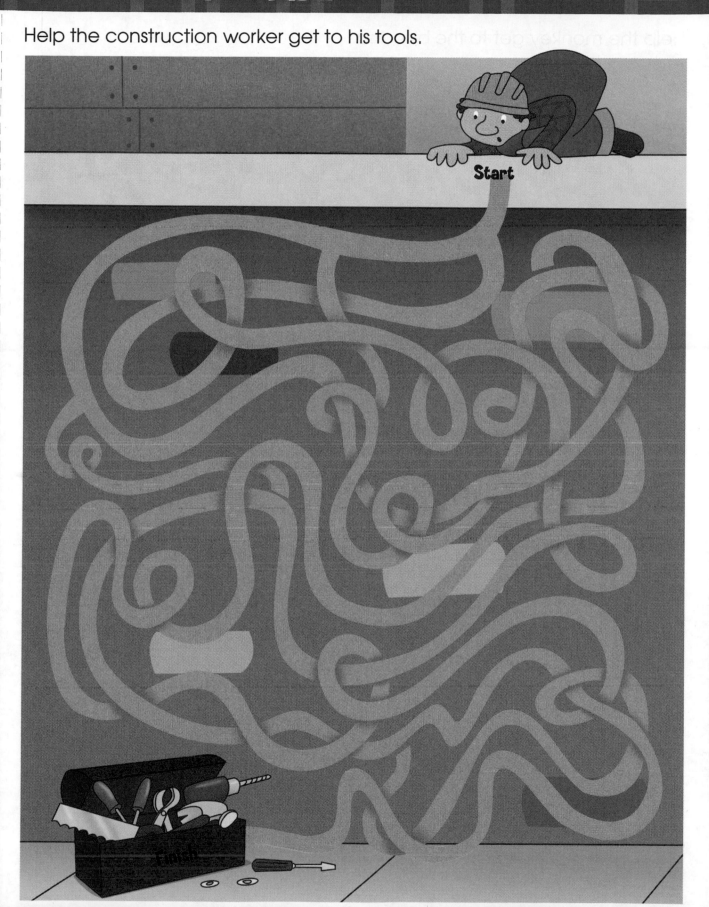

Start

Finish

Mazes

BANANA-RAMA

Help the monkey get to the banana.

Mazes

©School Zone Publishing Company 06328

HEAT WAVE

Follow the maze from start to finish.

Mazes

PLANET HOPPING

Help the alien get to its home.

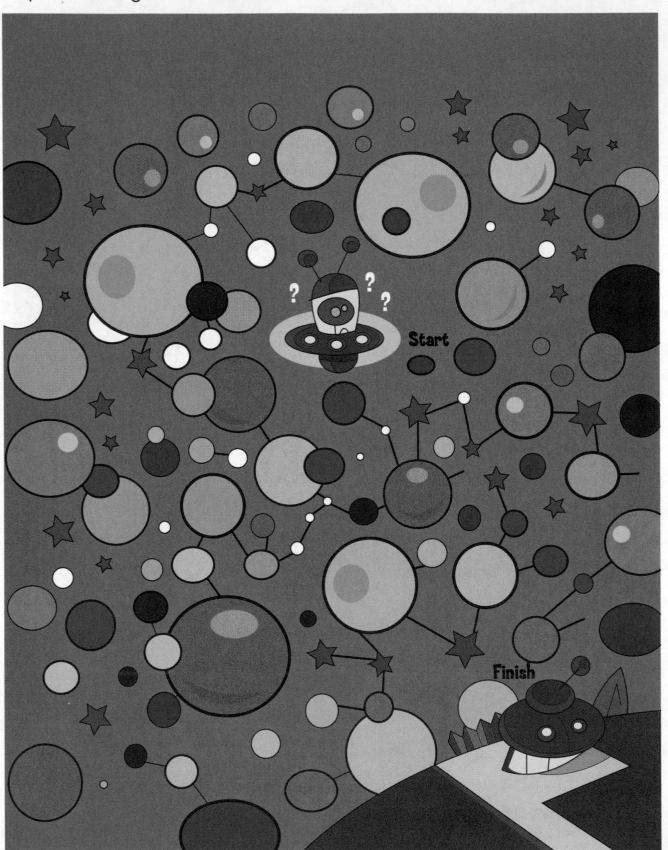

Mazes

©School Zone Publishing Company 06328

HIDDEN STARS

Follow the maze from start to finish.

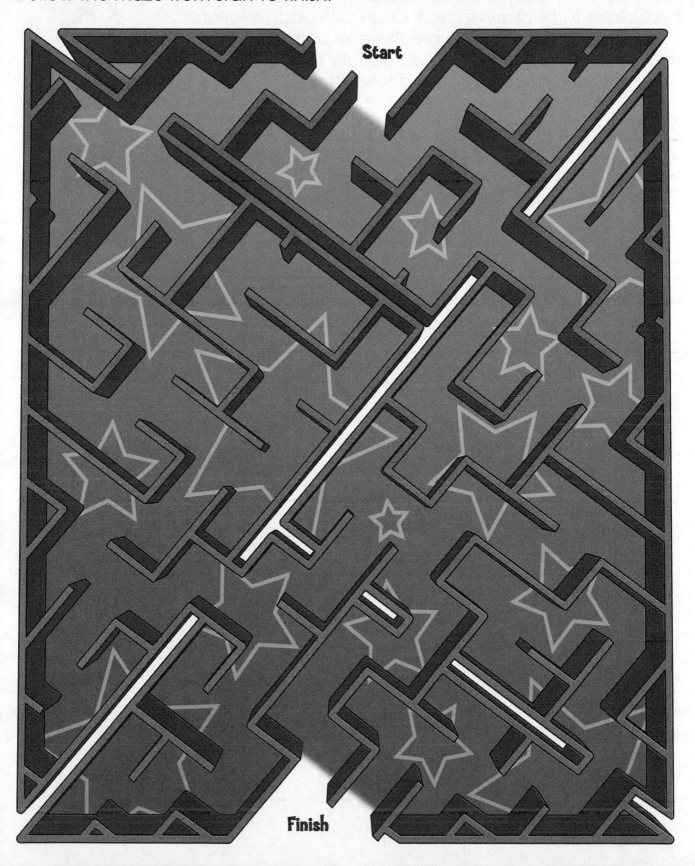

Start

Finish

Mazes

Choose which player will be X and which player will be O. Take turns drawing an X or an O in each section of the grid. Play until there are three Xs or three Os in a row horizontally, vertically, or diagonally or until the grid is filled. Whoever gets three in a row first wins!

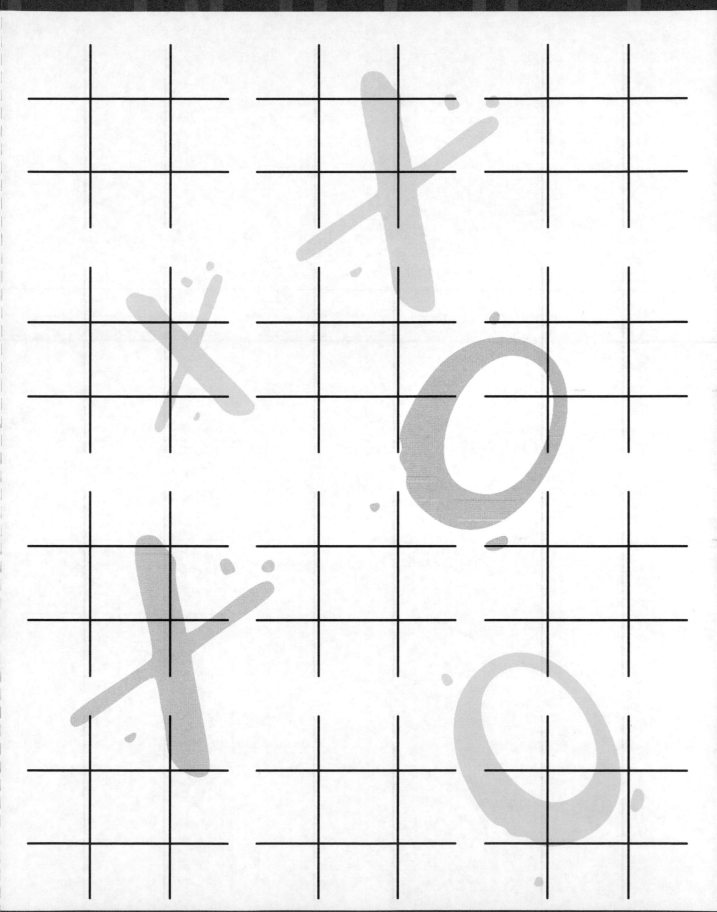

Tic-Tac-Toe

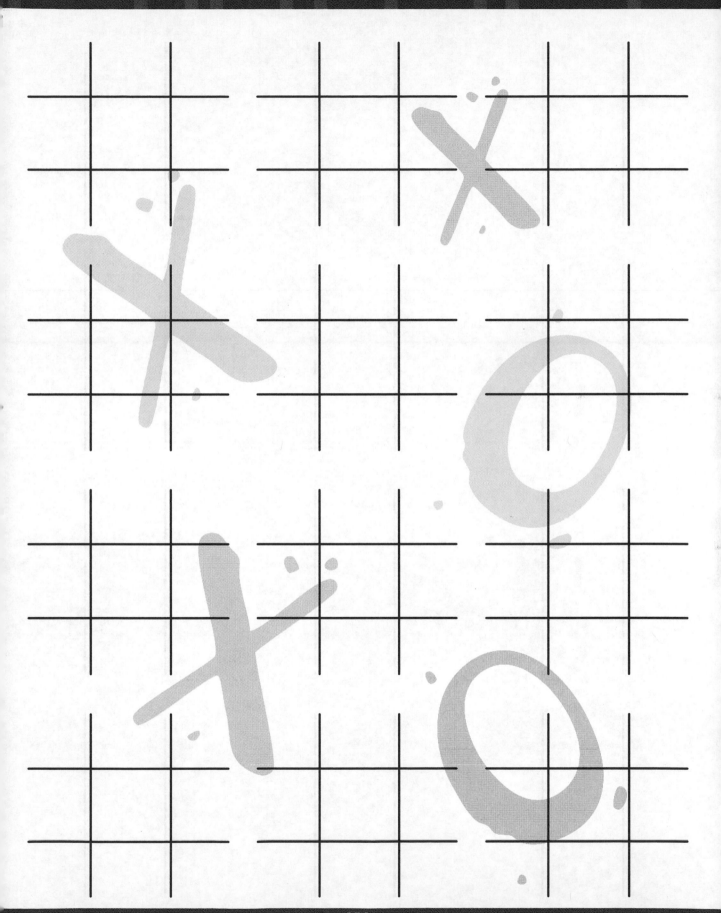

Tic-Tac-Toe

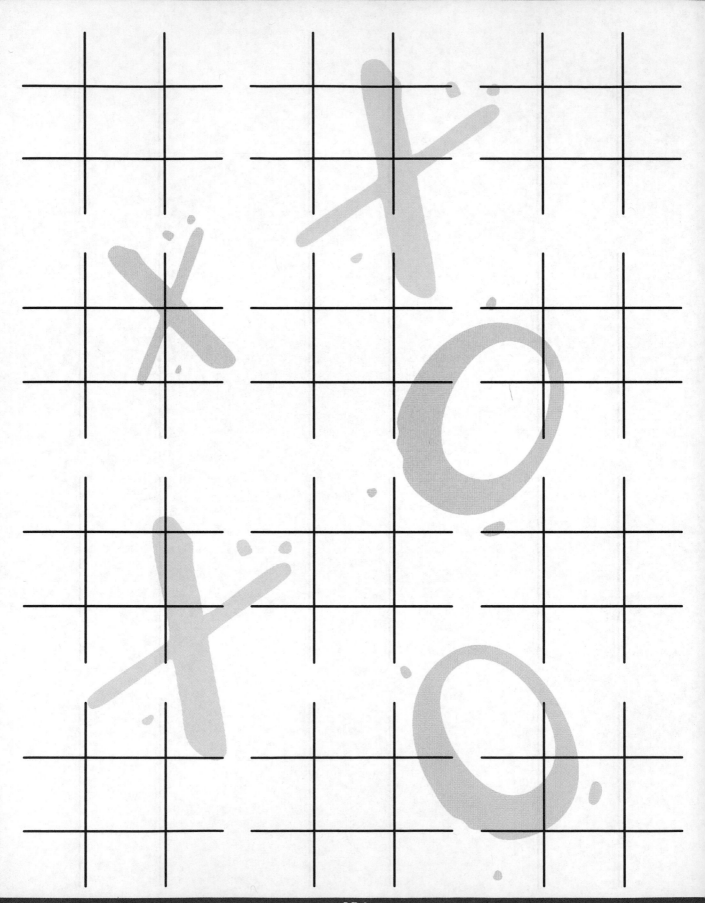

Tic-Tac-Toe

MOVING ALONG

Solve each math problem. Find the first answer on the grid. Draw a line to the second answer. Continue drawing lines to connect the answers in order. When you have finished, a picture will be revealed.

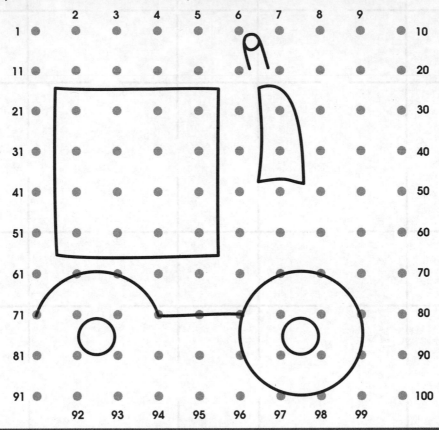

Line 1

1. 63 + 13 = _____

2. 99 - 33 = _____

3. 34 + 22 = _____

4. 75 - 29 = _____

5. 19 + 17 = _____

6. 56 - 30 = _____

7. 8 + 8 = _____

8. 48 - 31 = _____

9. 16 + 12 = _____

10. 74 - 36 = _____

11. 33 + 15 = _____

12. 87 - 38 = _____

13. 50 + 10 = _____

14. 89 - 19 = _____

15. 54 + 26 = _____

16. 84 - 5 = _____

Line 2

1. 61 + 13 = _____

2. 93 - 9 = _____

3. 80 + 13 = _____

4. 100 - 8 = _____

5. 45 + 36 = _____

6. 77 - 6 = _____

7. 48 + 13 = _____

8. 78 - 27 = _____

9. 33 + 8 = _____

10. 49 - 18 = _____

11. 17 + 4 = _____

12. 45 - 34 = _____

13. 8 + 4 = _____

14. 26 - 13 = _____

15. 9 + 5 = _____

16. 30 - 15 = _____

17. 9 + 7 = _____

Math Puzzle Grid

Color the picture below.

1 = **light yellow**   3 = **blue**   5 = **purple**   7 = **white**

2 = **orange**   4 = **dark blue**   6 = **black**

Color-by-Numbers

OFF TO SEA

Solve each math problem. Find the first answer on the grid. Draw a line to the second answer. Continue drawing lines to connect the answers in order. When you have finished, a picture will be revealed.

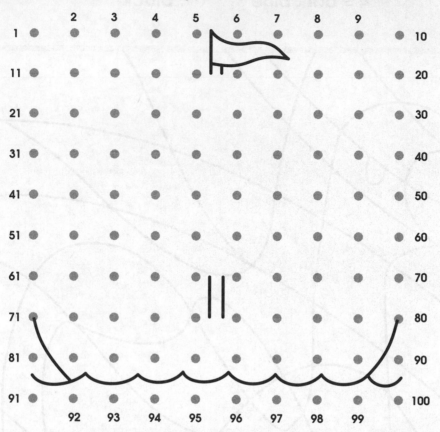

Line 1

1. 8 + 8 = _____

2. 25 - 10 = _____

3. 47 - 23 = _____

4. 30 + 3 = _____

5. 21 + 21 = _____

6. 81 - 30 = _____

7. 70 - 9 = _____

8. 45 + 17 = _____

9. 99 - 36 = _____

10. 55 + 9 = _____

11. 72 - 7 = _____

12. 40 + 26 = _____

13. 80 - 13 = _____

14. 34 + 34 = _____

15. 85 - 16 = _____

16. 50 + 20 = _____

17. 70 - 10 = _____

18. 42 + 7 = _____

19. 21 + 17 = _____

20. 15 + 12 = _____

21. 20 - 4 = _____

Line 2

1. 90 - 10 = _____

2. 62 + 17 = _____

3. 90 - 12 = _____

4. 65 + 12 = _____

5. 85 - 9 = _____

6. 53 + 22 = _____

7. 86 - 12 = _____

8. 56 + 17 = _____

9. 75 - 3 = _____

10. 40 + 31 = _____

Math Puzzle Grid

TIME TO HARVEST

Color the picture below.

1 = **yellow**　　3 = pink　　5 = **green**　　7 = **brown**　　9 = gray
2 = **red**　　4 = **blue**　　6 = **light brown**　　8 = white　　10 = **black**

©School Zone Publishing Company 06328　　　　　　Color-by-Numbers

Help the climber get to the top of the cliff.

Mazes

SILLY SEAL

Help Sal Seal get to the bucket of water.

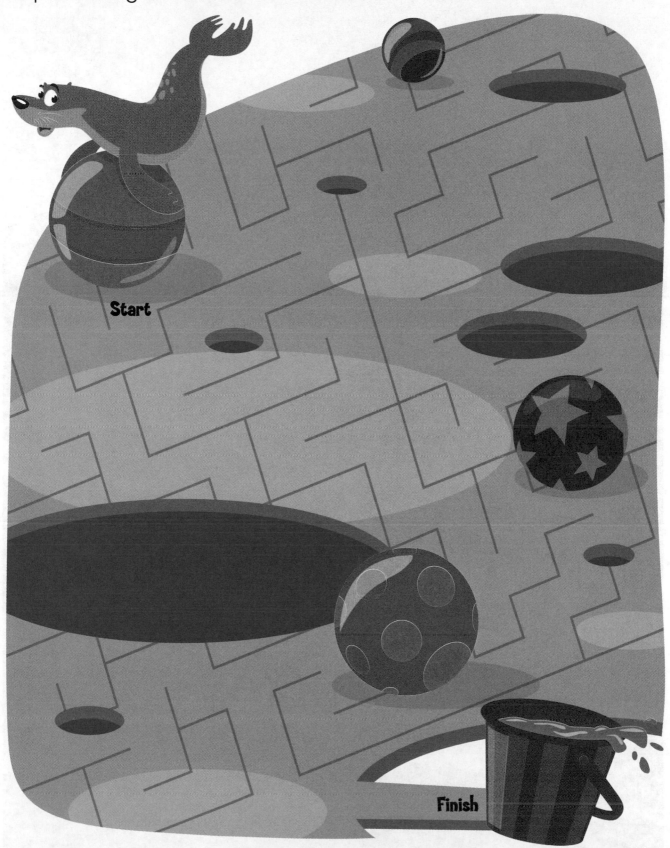

Start

Finish

Mazes

Help the man sink the eight ball.

THROUGH THE TUBES

Follow the maze from start to finish.

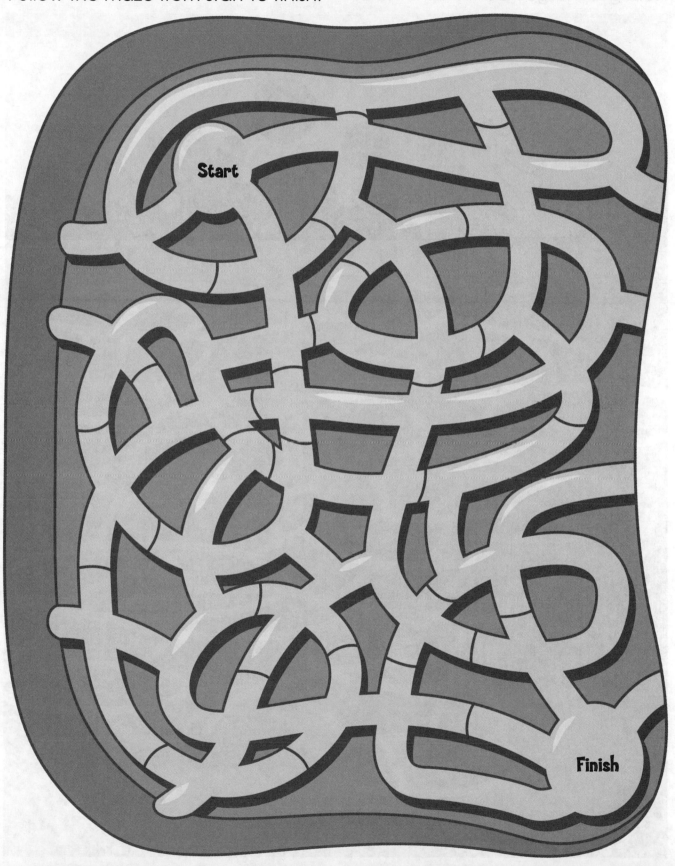

Mazes

PUTTING GREEN

Help get the golf ball into the hole.

Start

Finish

Mazes

©School Zone Publishing Company 06328

HENHOUSE

Help the hen and her chicks get home.

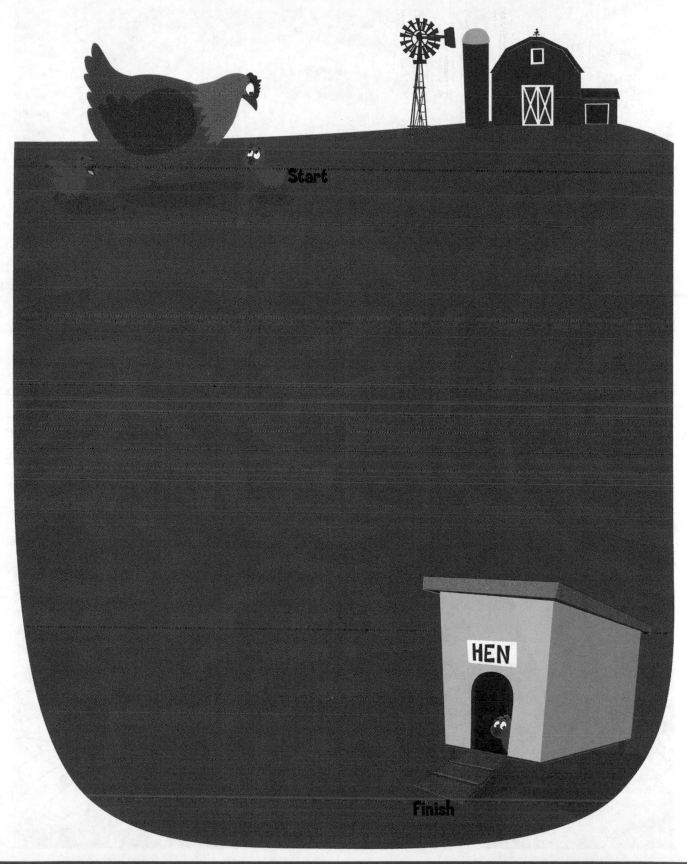

Start

HEN

Finish

Mazes

BUZZING BEE

Help the bee get to the beehive.

Start

Finish

Mazes

ON THE RUNWAY

Help the plane get to the gate.

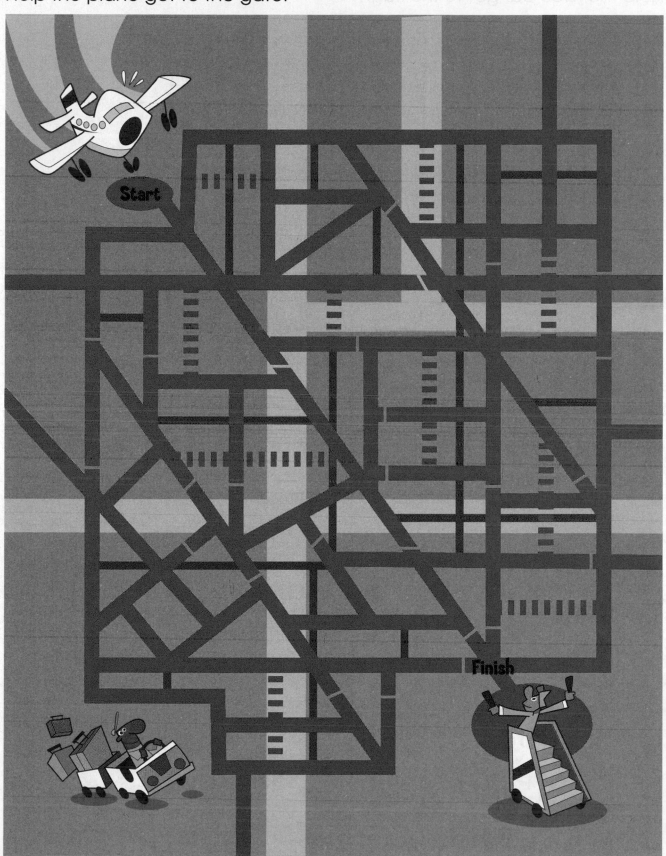

Mazes

Help the race car get to the flag.

Start

Finish

Mazes

©School Zone Publishing Company 06328

WHICH WAY DO WE GO?

Follow the maze from start to finish.

Start

Finish

Mazes

OUT FOR A STROLL

Help the dog get to the fire hydrant.

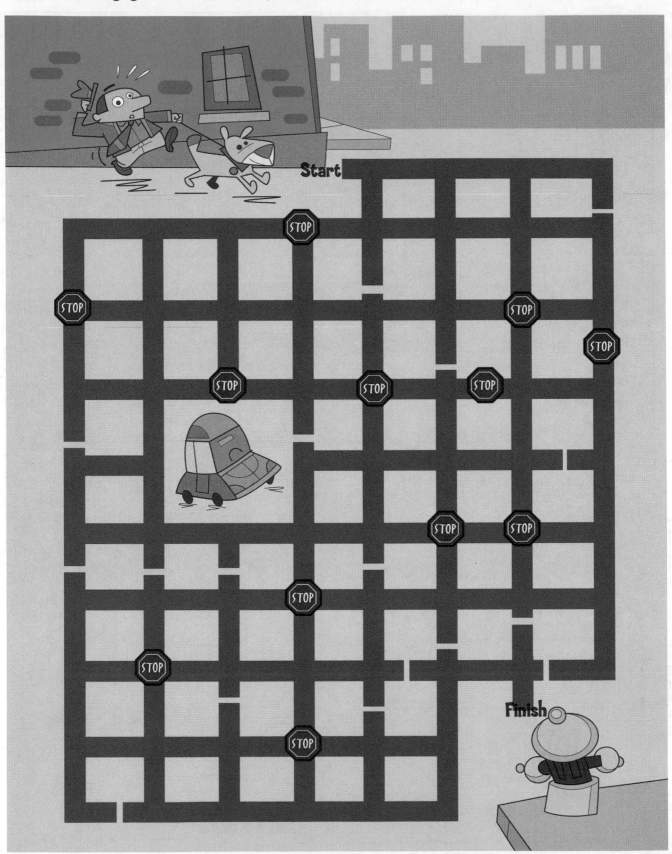

Mazes

MAKING A FIELD GOAL

Help the kicker get the football through the uprights.

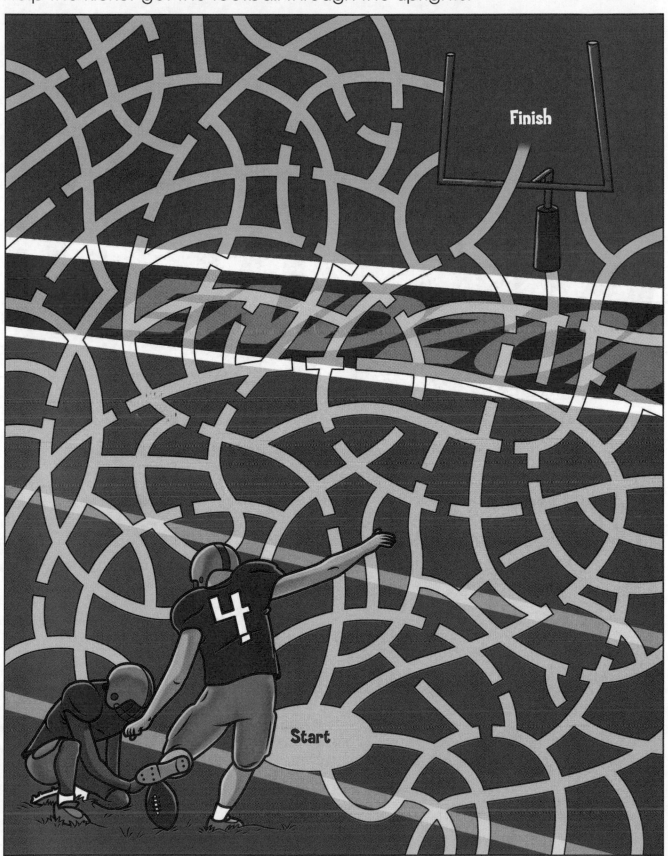

Mazes

ROUND AND ROUND

Follow the maze from start to finish.

Mazes

IN THE LABORATORY

Help the scientist with his experiment.

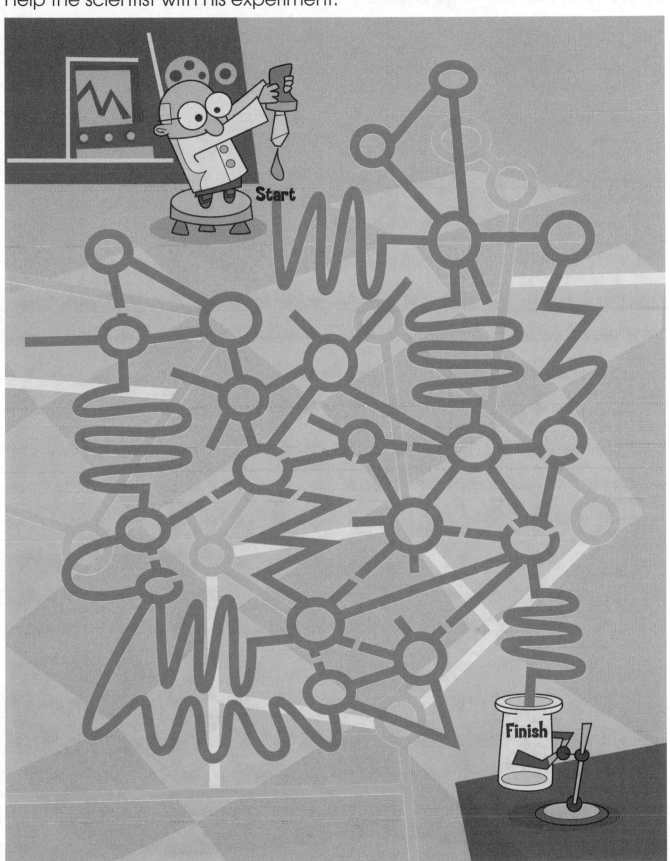

©School Zone Publishing Company 06328

Mazes

FISH FAMILY

Help Father Fish get to his children.

Start

Finish

Mazes

BEST BUDDIES

Help Parker Pony get to the cowboy.

Start

Finish

Mazes

BIRDS OF A FEATHER

Help the cockatoo get to the toucan.

Start

Finish

Mazes

CHAINED UP

Follow the maze from start to finish.

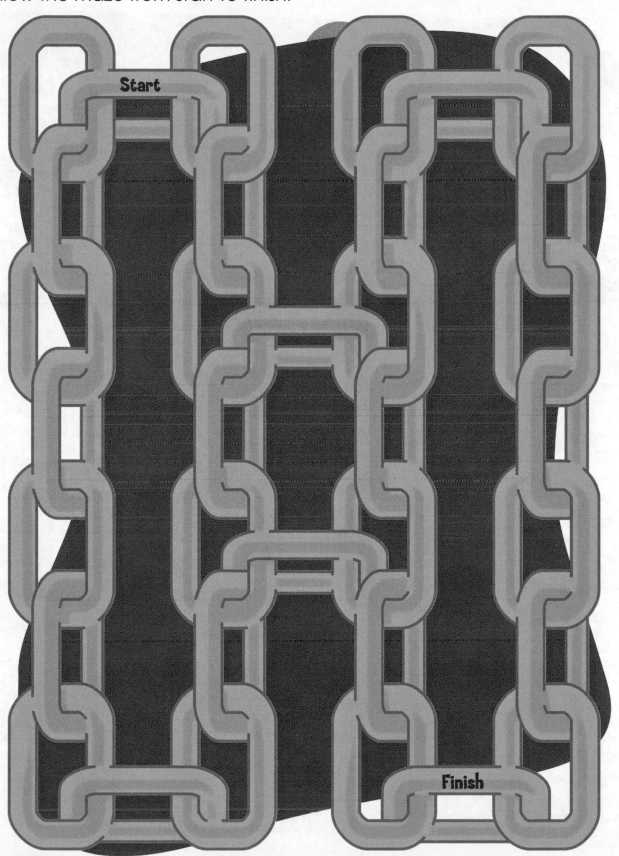

Start

Finish

Mazes

A DAY AT THE MUSEUM

Help the guard protect the painting.

Start

Finish

Mazes

ON THE FIELD

Help get the ball into the goal.

Mazes

Follow the maze from start to finish.

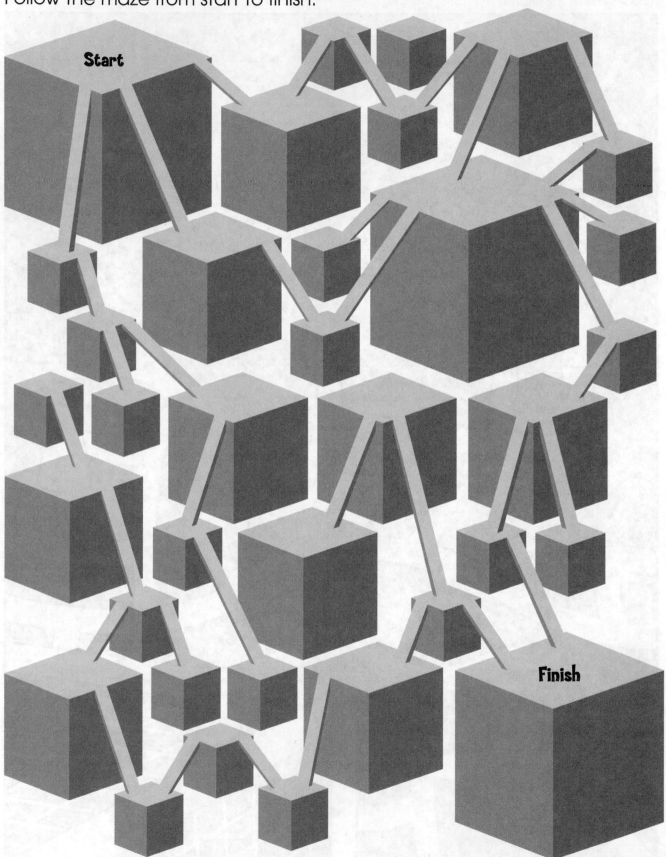

Start

Finish

TURNING THE CORNER

Follow the maze from start to finish.

Start

Finish

©School Zone Publishing Company 06328

Mazes

NOTEPAD

Help the pencil draw a path to the bottom of the page.

Start

Finish

Mazes

OUT OF FOCUS

Help the boy find his glasses.

Start

Finish

Mazes

CIRCLE GARDEN

Follow the maze from start to finish.

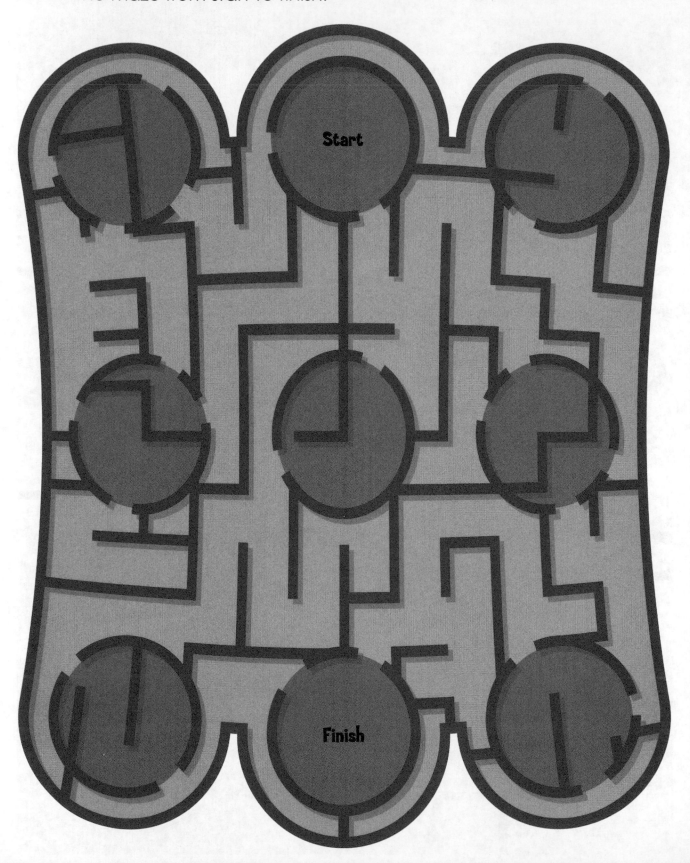

DON'T GET CAUGHT!

Help Shawn Shark swim through the net.

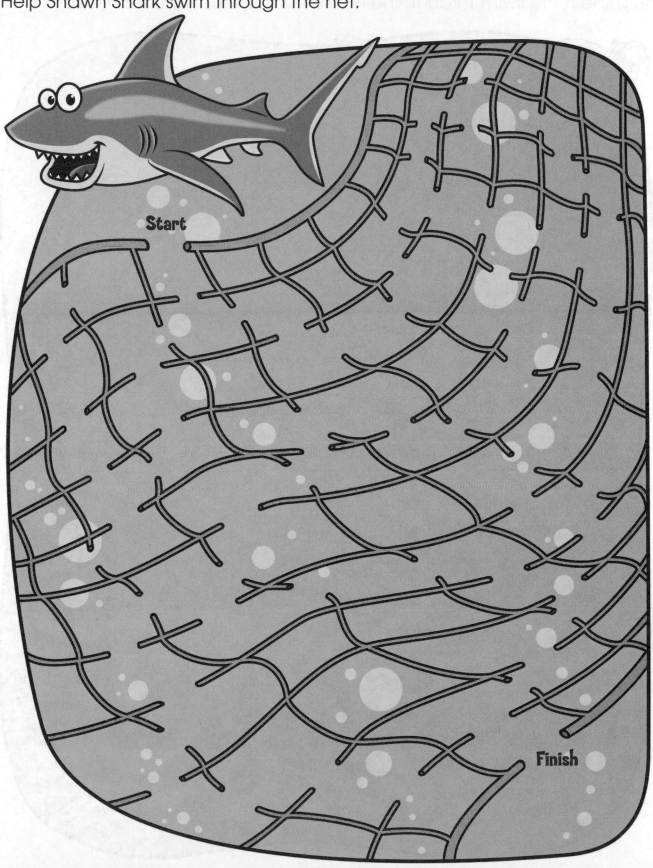

Mazes

JELLYFISH JUMBLE

Help the turtle swim through the jellyfish. Don't touch the tentacles!

Start

Finish

Mazes

CIRCLE AROUND

Follow the maze from start to finish.

Mazes

A SNAKE'S SNACK

Help Sandra Snake get to the bunch of grapes.

Start

Finish

SQUARE BURST

Follow the maze from start to finish.

Start

Finish

Mazes

LOOK OUT BELOW!

Help the ambulance get to the man.

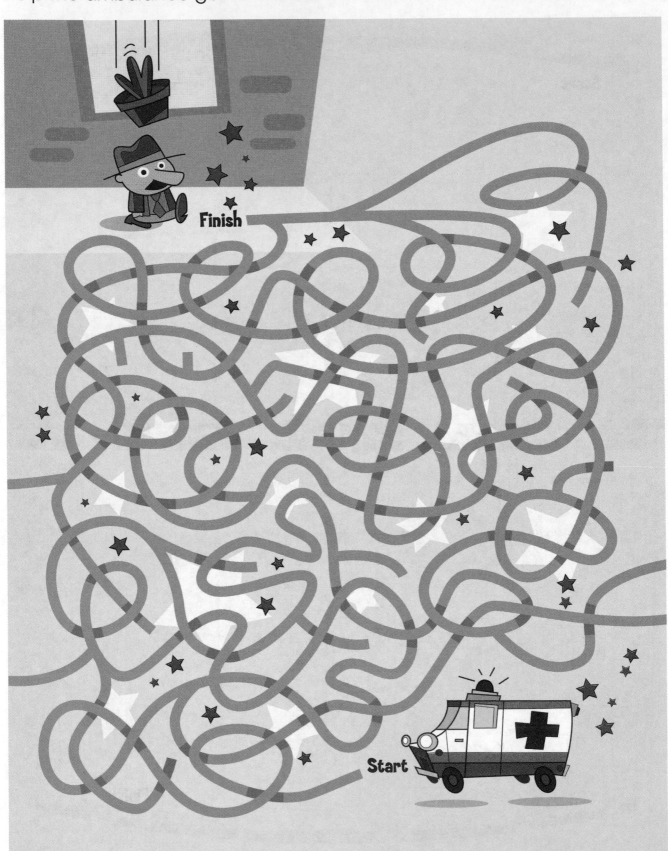

PAPER PEOPLE

Follow the maze from start to finish.

Start

Finish

Mazes

JUST HOPPING BY

Help Kacy Koala get to Keegan Kangaroo.

Start

Finish

Mazes

Follow the maze from start to finish.

Start

Finish

Mazes

TOUCHDOWN!

Help the player in red make a touchdown.

Start

Finish

Mazes

ORANGE OBSTACLES

Follow the maze from start to finish.

Start

Finish

Mazes

ROUND AND AROUND YOU GO!

Follow the arrows through the maze to get from start to finish.

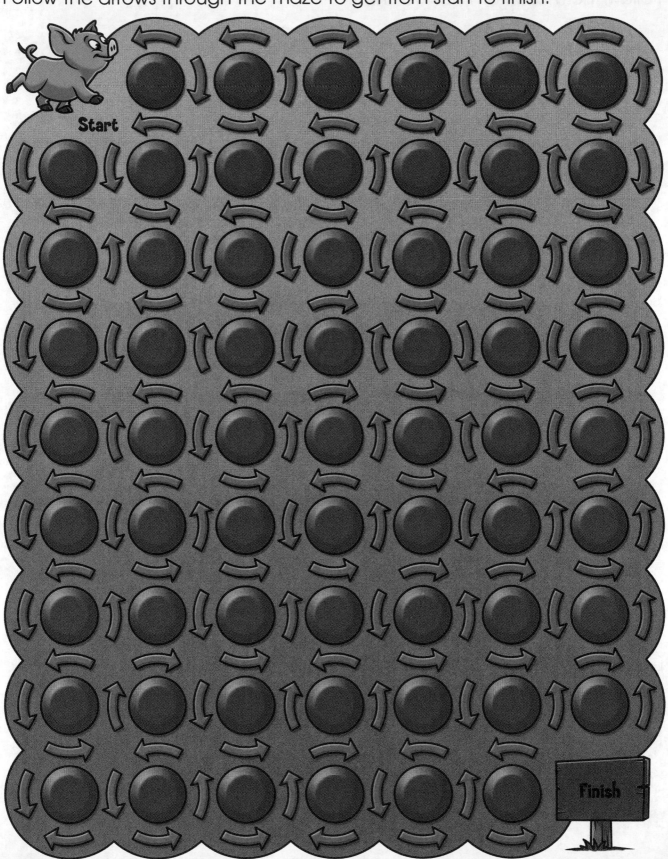

Start

Finish

MAGNETIC FORCE

Follow the maze from start to finish.

Start

Finish

Mazes

THROUGH THE LEAVES

Follow the maze from start to finish.

Start

Finish

Mazes

TALL AND SHORT

Help George Giraffe get to Zeb Zebra.

Start

Finish

Mazes

Follow the maze from start to finish.

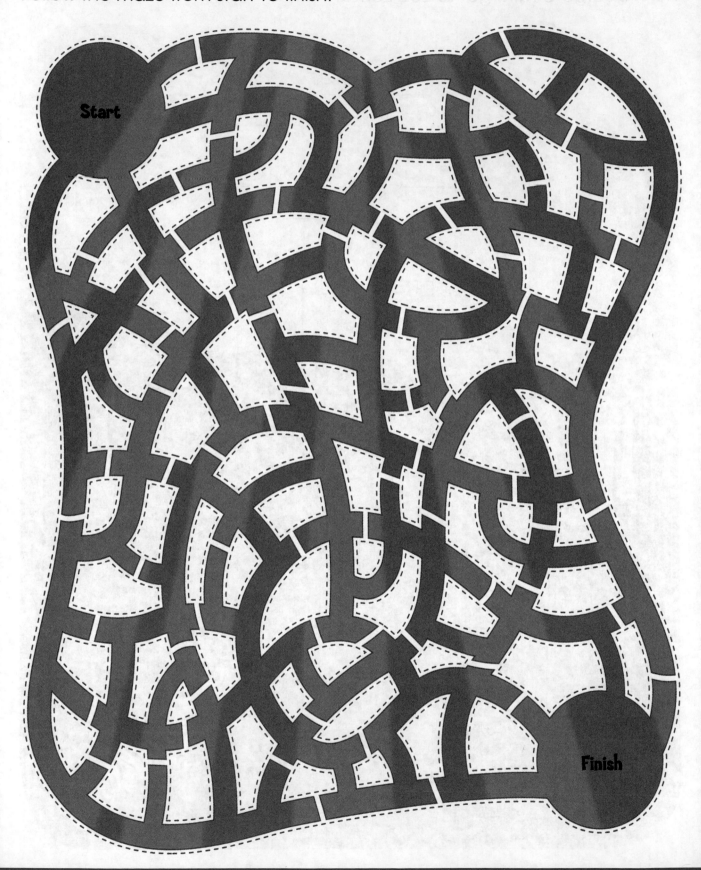

Start

Finish

Mazes

BOXED IN

In this game, try to complete the most squares. Each player takes a turn drawing a vertical or horizontal line between two dots. When you complete a square, write your first initial in it. You then can take another turn. Your turn can include forming several boxes. A single line may form more than one box. Your turn is over when you draw a line that does not form a box.

The game ends when all of the possible boxes have been formed and filled. The winner is the player with the most initialed boxes.

©School Zone Publishing Company 06328

BOXED IN

See page 201 for directions.

Boxed In   ©School Zone Publishing Company 06328

BOXED IN

See page 201 for directions.

Boxed In

BOXED IN

See page 201 for directions.

BOXED IN

See page 201 for directions.

Boxed In

BOXED IN

See page 201 for directions.

©School Zone Publishing Company 06328

HANGMAN

In this game, one person thinks of a word and draws the same number of dashes as letters in the word. The other player guesses the letters. If a guess is right, the letter is written on the correct dash or dashes. If the guess is wrong, a body is drawn one part at a time (a complete body includes a head, a torso, two legs, two arms, two hands, and two feet). The object is to guess the word before the drawing is finished.

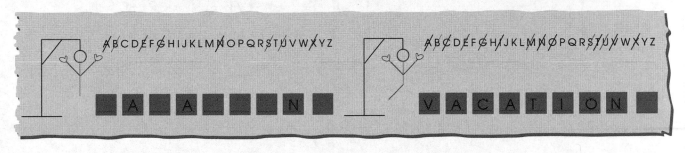

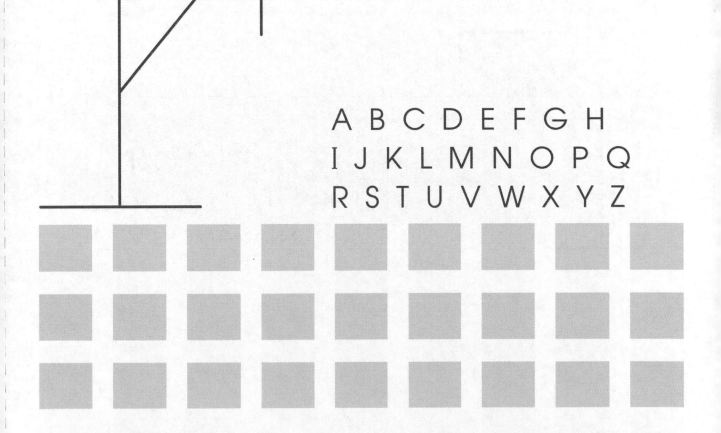

©School Zone Publishing Company 06328

HANGMAN

See page 207 for directions.

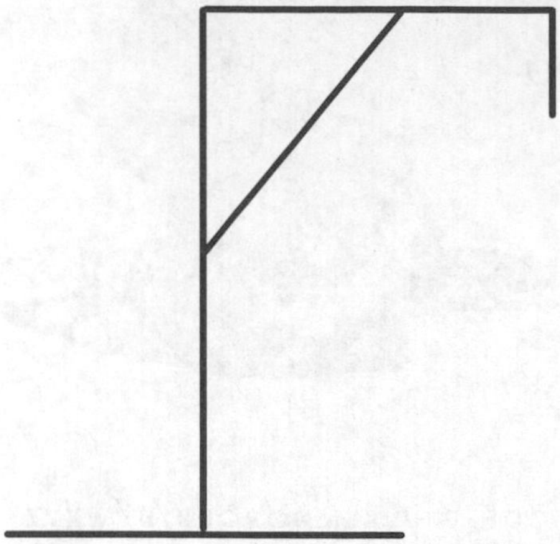

A B C D E F G H
I J K L M N O P Q
R S T U V W X Y Z

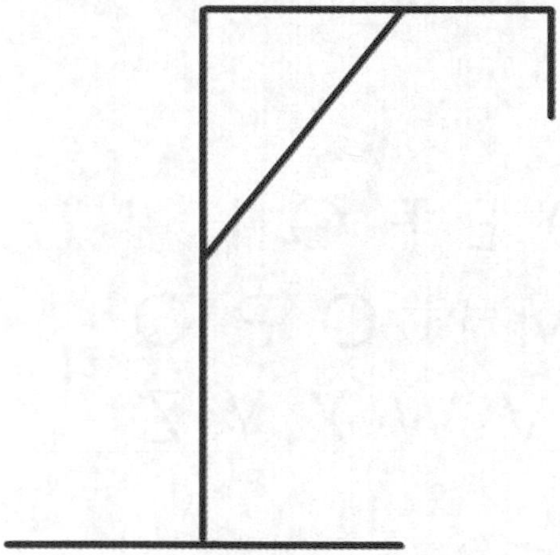

A B C D E F G H
I J K L M N O P Q
R S T U V W X Y Z

HANGMAN

See page 207 for directions.

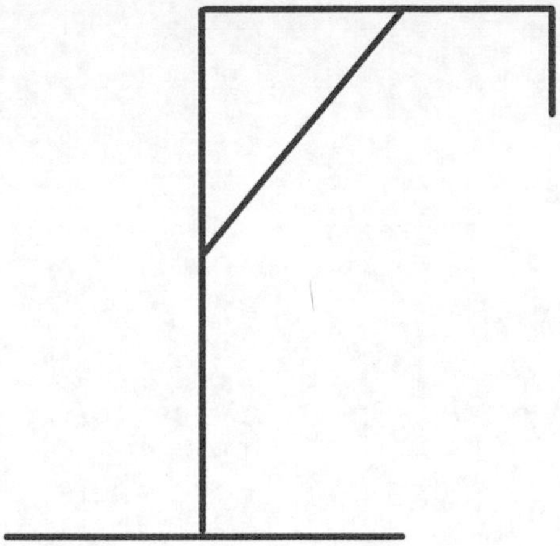

A B C D E F G H
I J K L M N O P Q
R S T U V W X Y Z

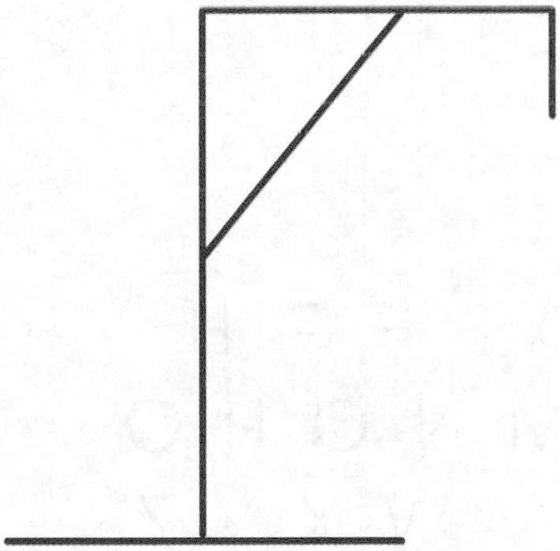

A B C D E F G H
I J K L M N O P Q
R S T U V W X Y Z

Hangman

HANGMAN

See page 207 for directions.

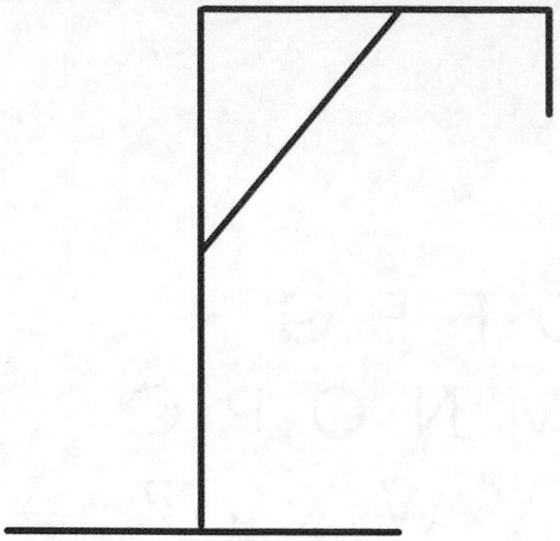

A B C D E F G H
I J K L M N O P Q
R S T U V W X Y Z

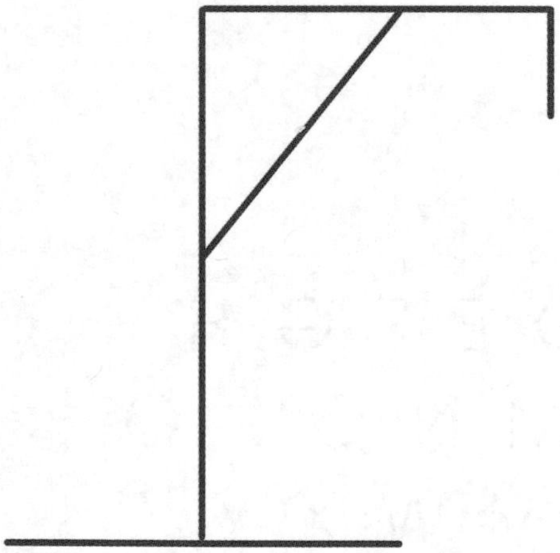

A B C D E F G H
I J K L M N O P Q
R S T U V W X Y Z

Follow the maze from start to finish.

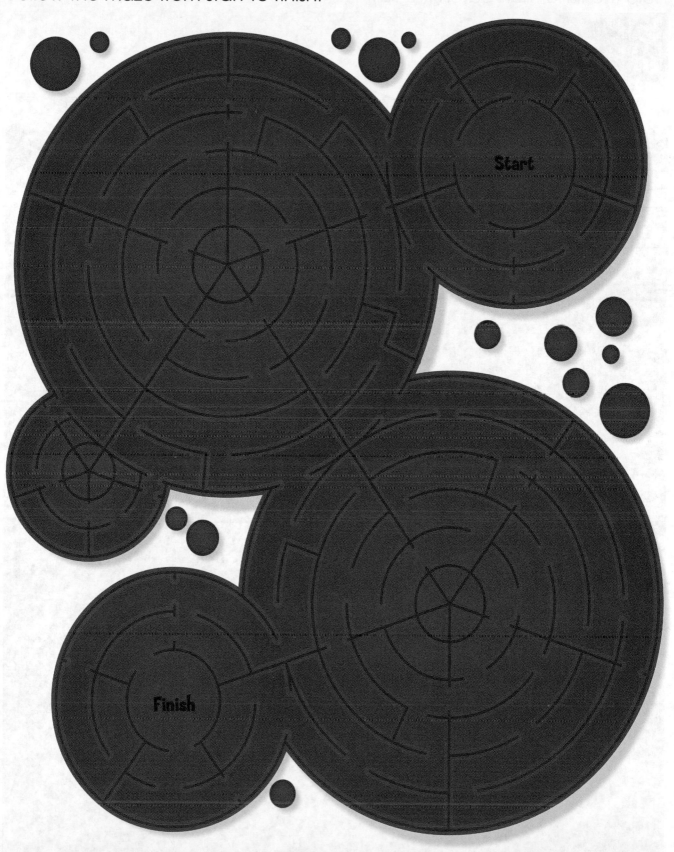

Mazes

GONE FISHING

Help the fisherman catch the fish.

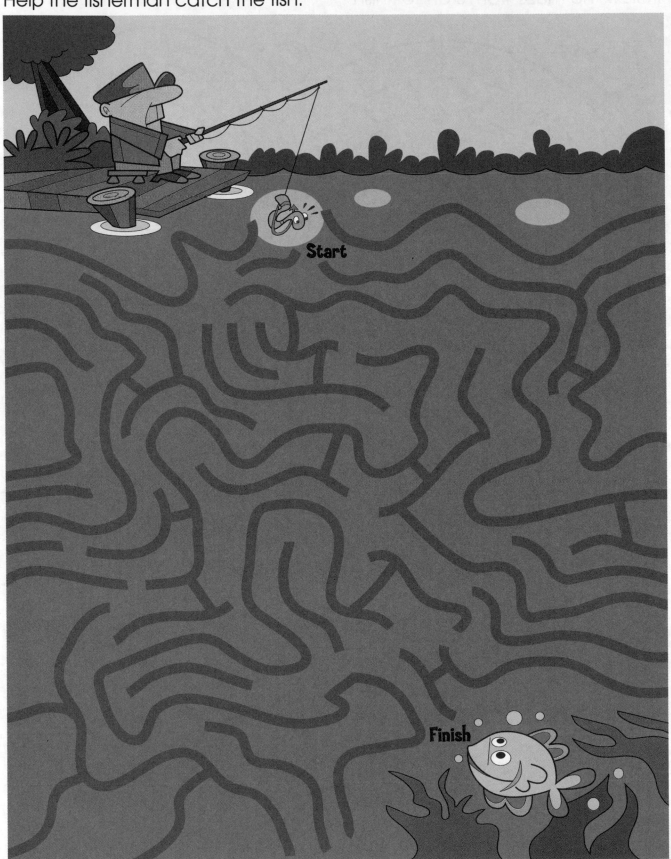

Start

Finish

Mazes

WATERMELON SURPRISE

Follow the maze from start to finish.

Mazes

DOWN UNDER

Help the worm get to his underground home.

Start

Finish

DON'T BUG ME!

Help the praying mantis get to the ladybug.

Start

Finish

Mazes

SEEING STARS

Help the mother bird get to the nest.

CIRCLES GALORE

Follow the maze from start to finish.

Mazes

PLATFORM HOPPING

Follow the maze from start to finish.

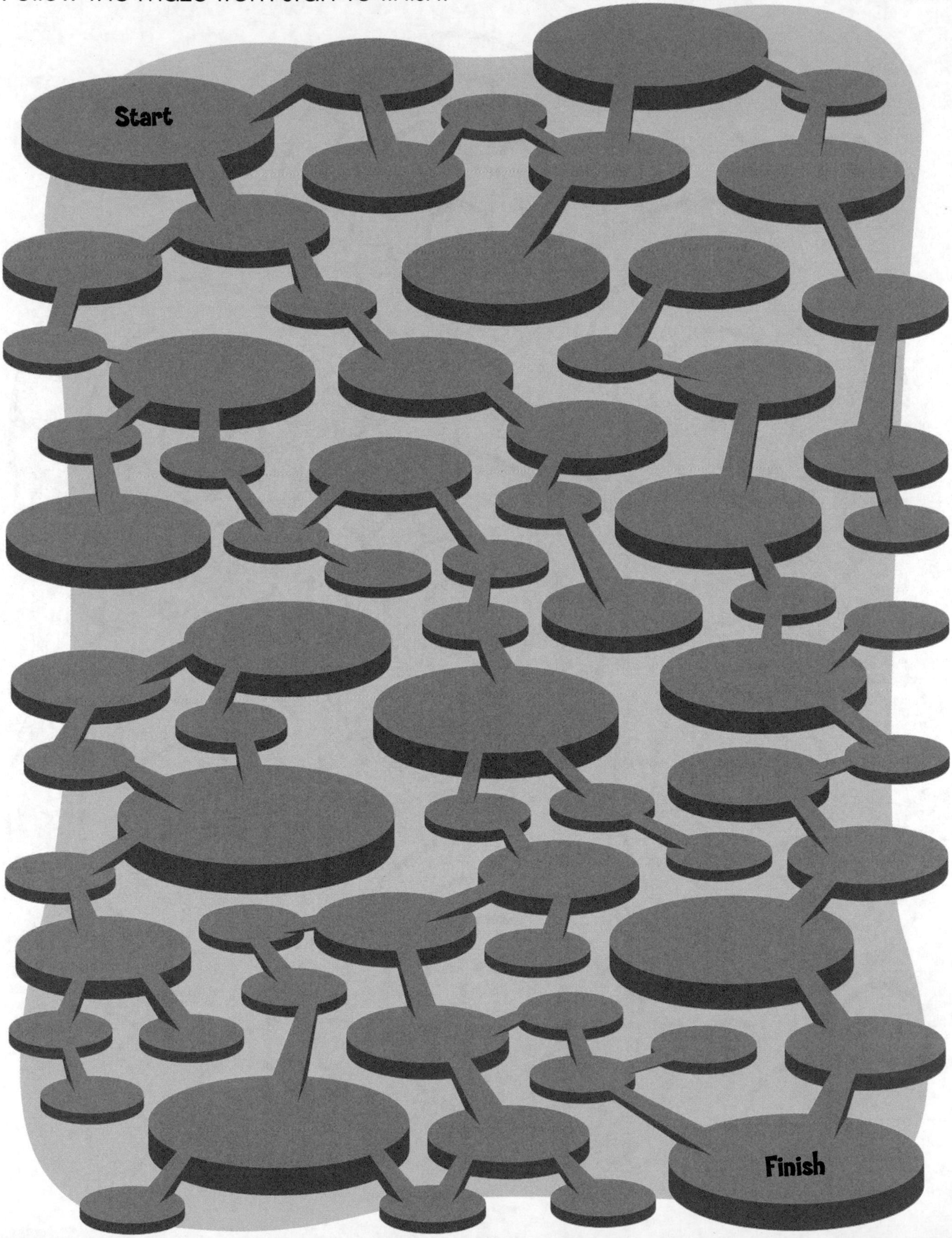

Start

Finish

BUBBLE GUM

Follow the maze from start to finish.

Start

Finish

Mazes

CAT AND MOUSE

Help the mouse get away from the cat.

RACING TO THE FIRE

Help the fire truck get to the fire.

Mazes

WHERE IS MY SHOE?

Help the boy get to his shoe.

Start

Finish

THE BLUE WALL

Follow the maze from start to finish.

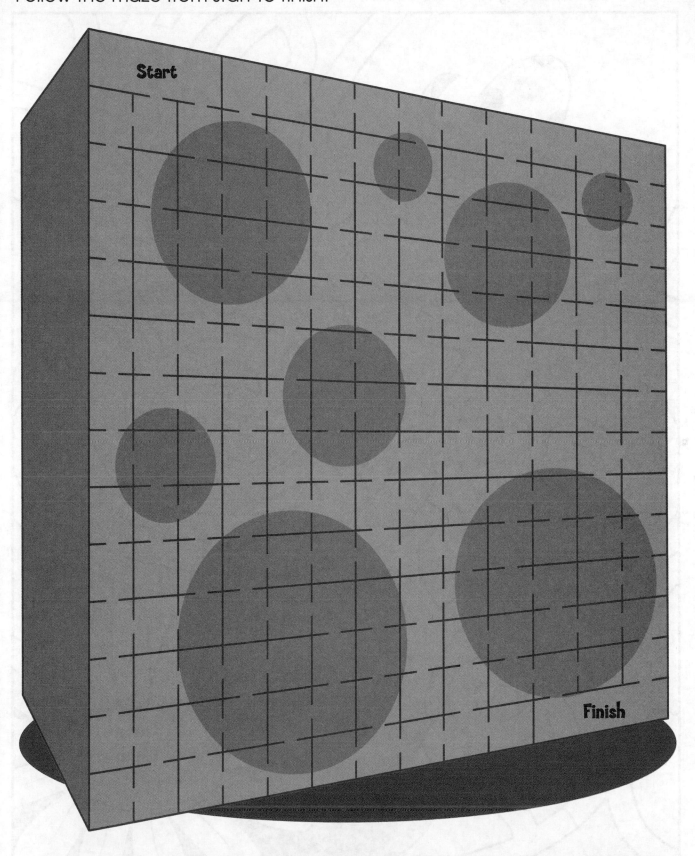

Mazes

FLYING AROUND

Help the ladybug get to the flower.

Start

Finish

Mazes

TIRE TREAD

Follow the maze from start to finish.

Mazes

ROCK CLIMBING

Help the climber get to the top of the cliff.

Mazes

OBSTACLE COURSE

Follow the maze from start to finish.

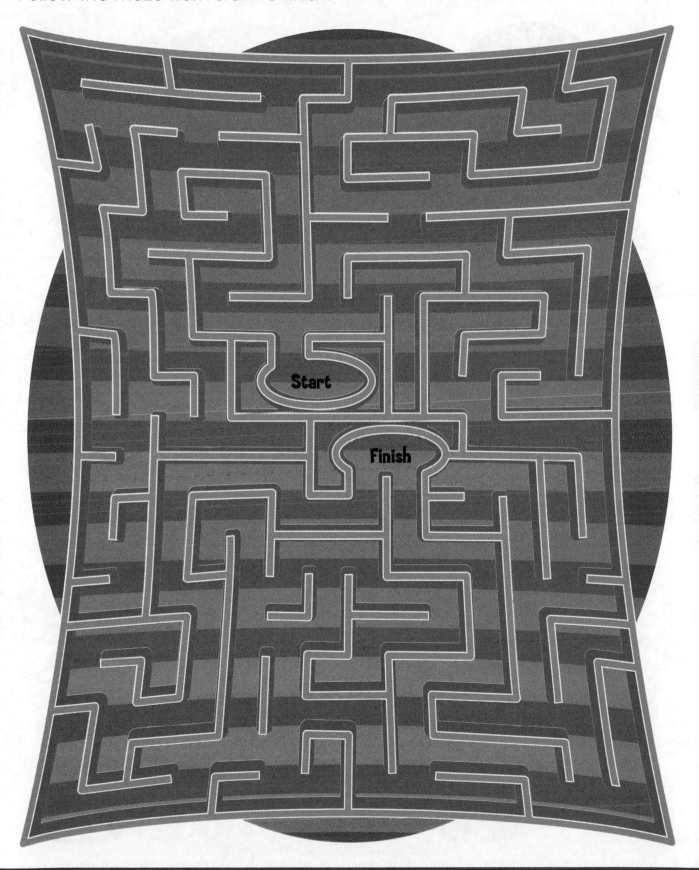

Mazes

DIVING DUO

Help Olivia Octopus get to the scuba diving salamander.

Start

Finish

Mazes   ©School Zone Publishing Company 06328

ORANGE WAVE

Follow the maze from start to finish.

Mazes

Help Riley Rabbit visit Haley Hippo.

TWEET, TWEET

Help Betty Bird get to her tree.

Start

Finish

Mazes

PURPLE QUILT

Follow the maze from start to finish.

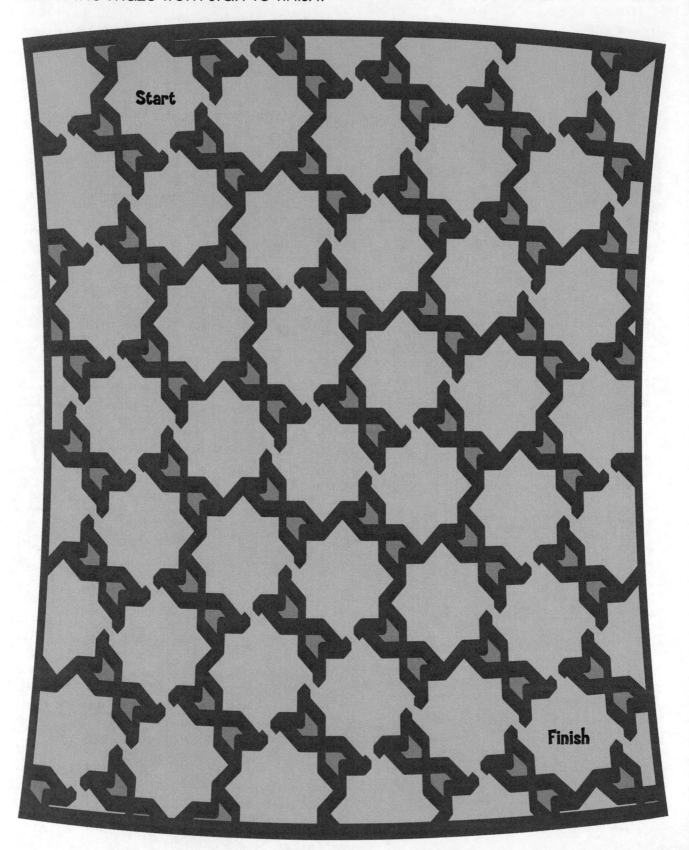

Mazes

TURKEY TIME

Help Tiffany Turkey find her egg.

Mazes

AQUA WORLD

Follow the maze from start to finish.

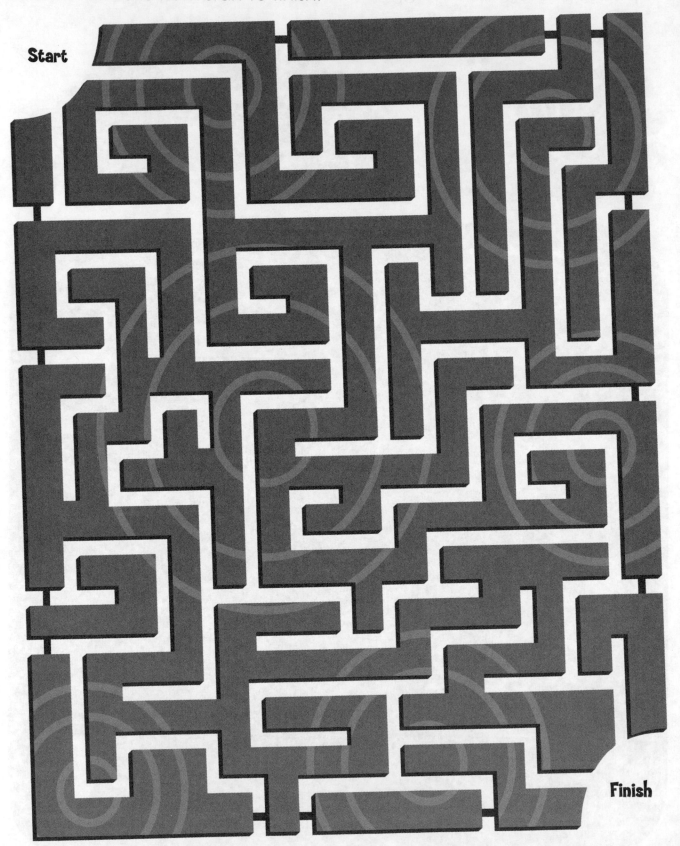

Start

Finish

HORSE HURDLES

Follow the arrows through the maze to get from start to finish.

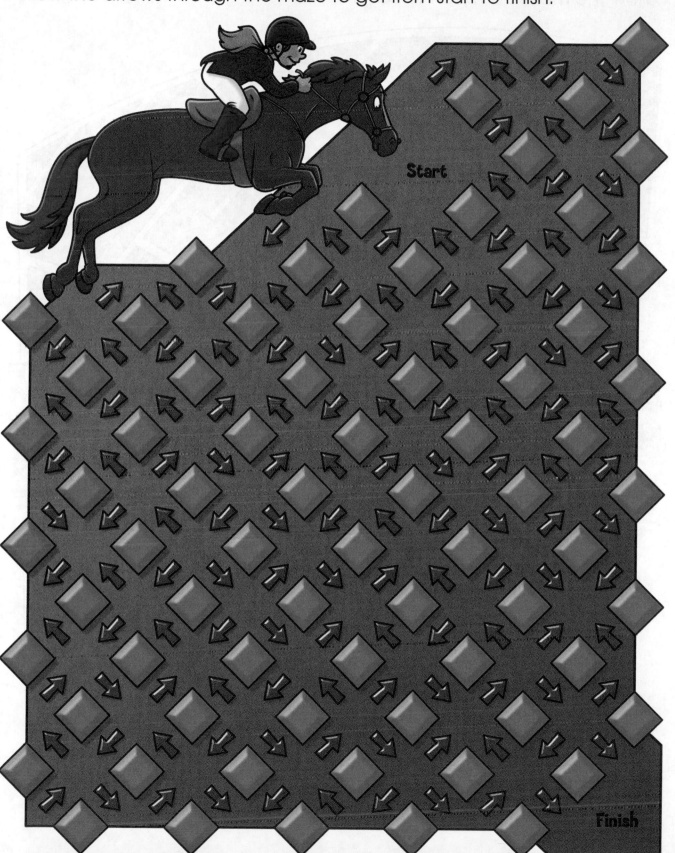

Start

Finish

Mazes

LUCKY STARS

Follow the maze from start to finish.

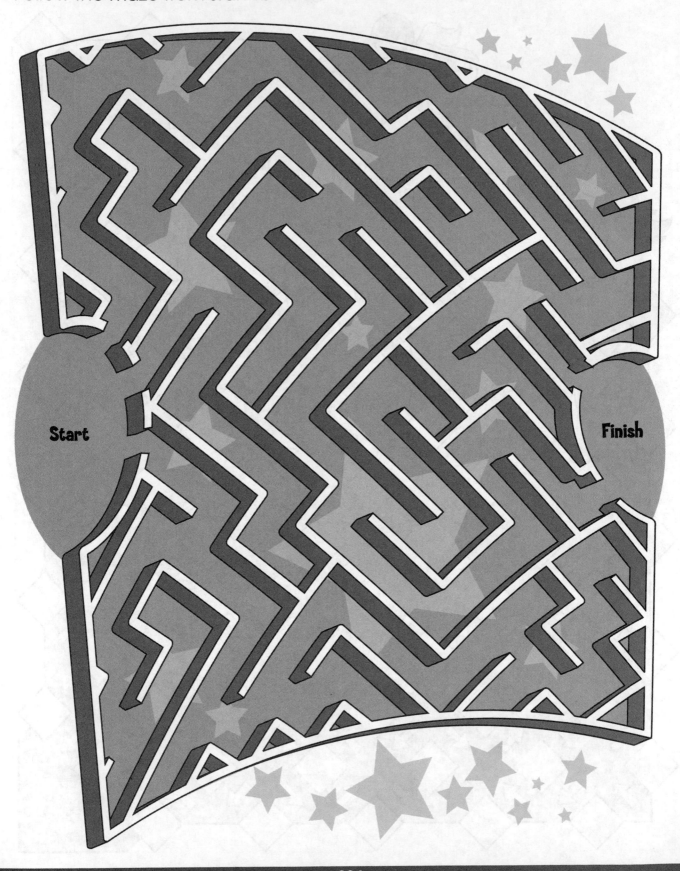

Start

Finish

SQUEAKY ROBOT

Follow the arrows through the maze to get from start to finish.

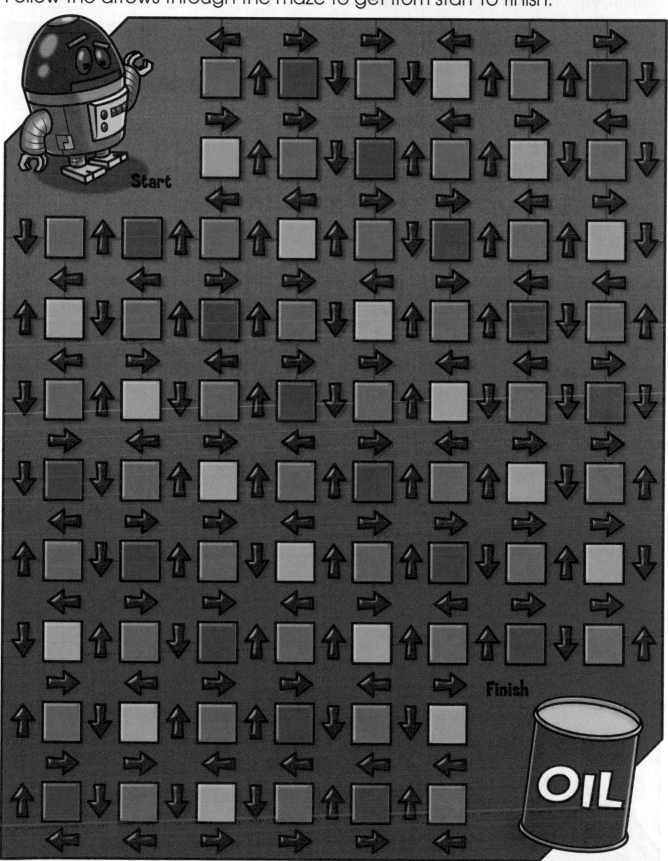

Start

Finish

Mazes

Help the polar bear get to the other side of the iceberg.

OUT AT SEA

Help Wilma Whale get to Margo Mouse.

Mazes

REPAIR SHOP

Help the robot get to the tools he needs.

Start

Finish

BEEHIVE

Follow the maze from start to finish.

Start

Finish

Mazes

Help the spider find his glasses.

TRANSFORMATION

Help the caterpillar get to the butterfly.

Start

Finish

Mazes

NOSEY

Help the snowman find his carrot nose.

Mazes

IN STITCHES

Follow the maze from start to finish.

Start

Finish

Mazes

MR. LONG NECK

Help the giraffe get through the forest.

Mazes
©School Zone Publishing Company 06328

GREEN HEDGE

Follow the maze from start to finish.

Start

Finish

Mazes

CIRCUIT BOARD

Follow the maze from start to finish.

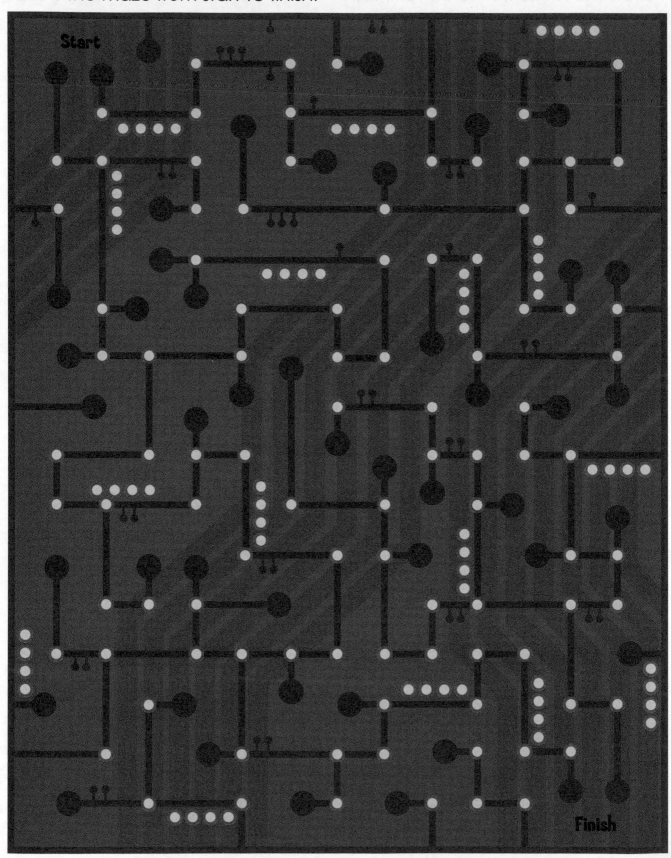

TOY MICE

Follow the maze from start to finish.

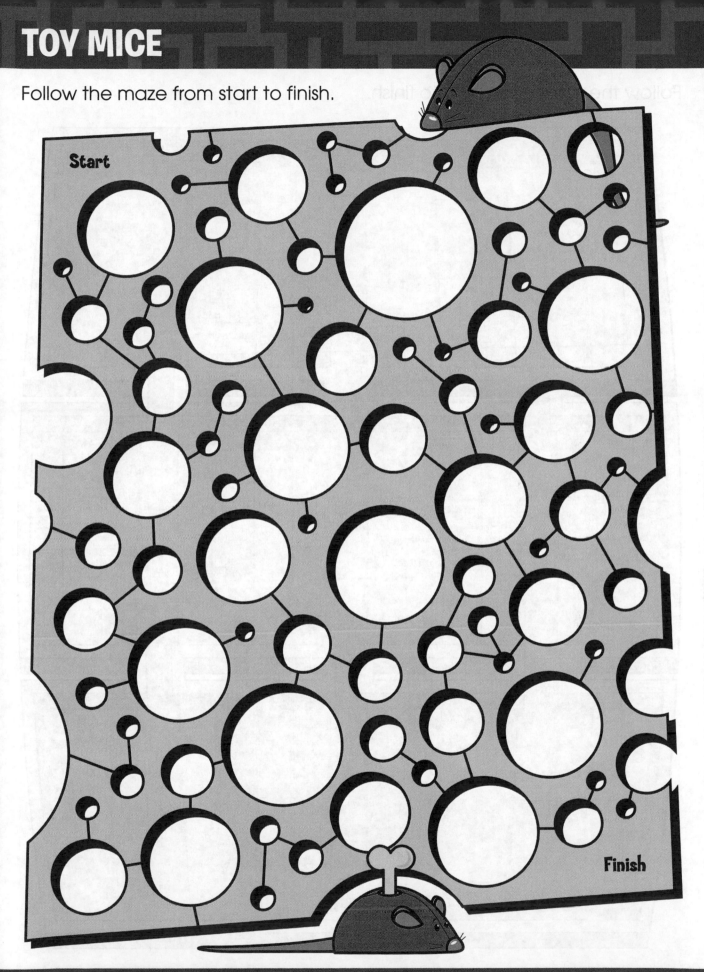

Start

Finish

Mazes

OLYMPIC-SIZE POOL

Follow the maze from start to finish.

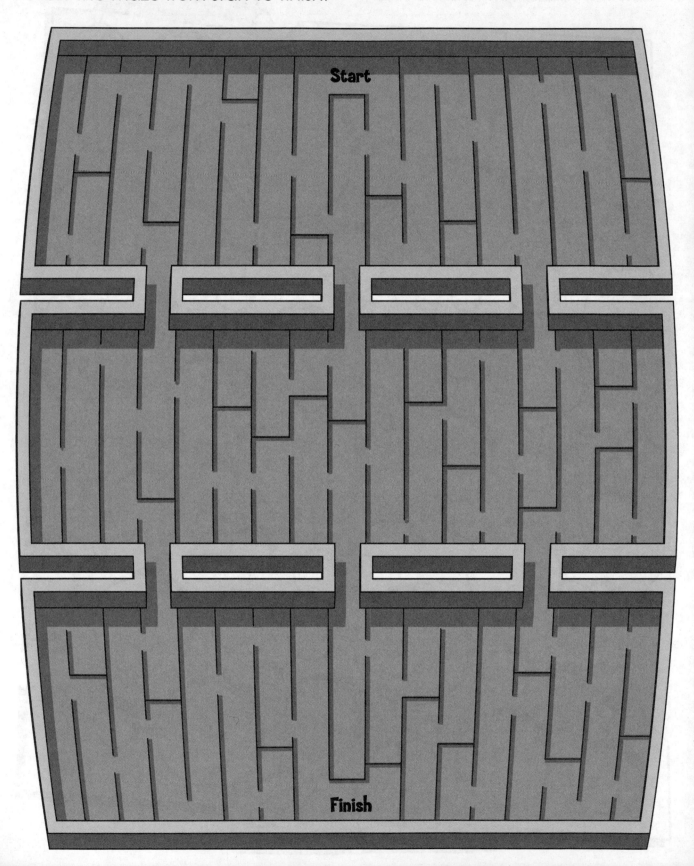

Start

Finish

Mazes

A LONG WAY DOWN

Help the hiker get to the ledge.

Start

Finish

Mazes

HOME BY THE SEA

Help the hermit crab get to the sandcastle.

Start

Finish

Mazes

ZIG ZAG

Follow the maze from start to finish.

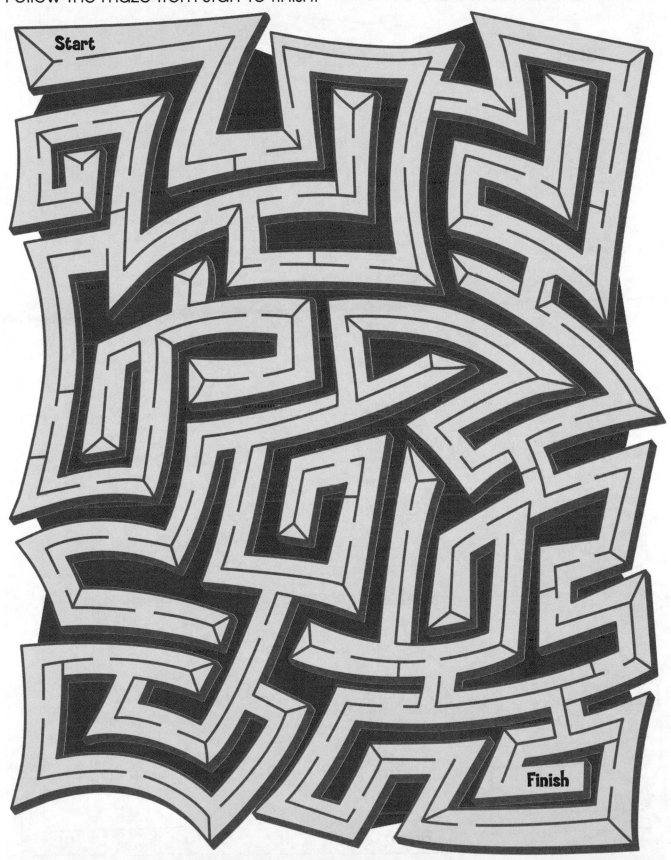

Start

Finish

Mazes

WACKY WALLS!

Follow the maze from start to finish.

Start

Finish

ITSY, BITSY ROBOT SPIDER

Follow the maze from start to finish.

Mazes

CHEMISTRY SET

Follow the maze from start to finish.

Start

Finish

Mazes

OFF THE WALL

Follow the maze from start to finish.

Mazes

PURPLE PATH

Follow the maze from start to finish.

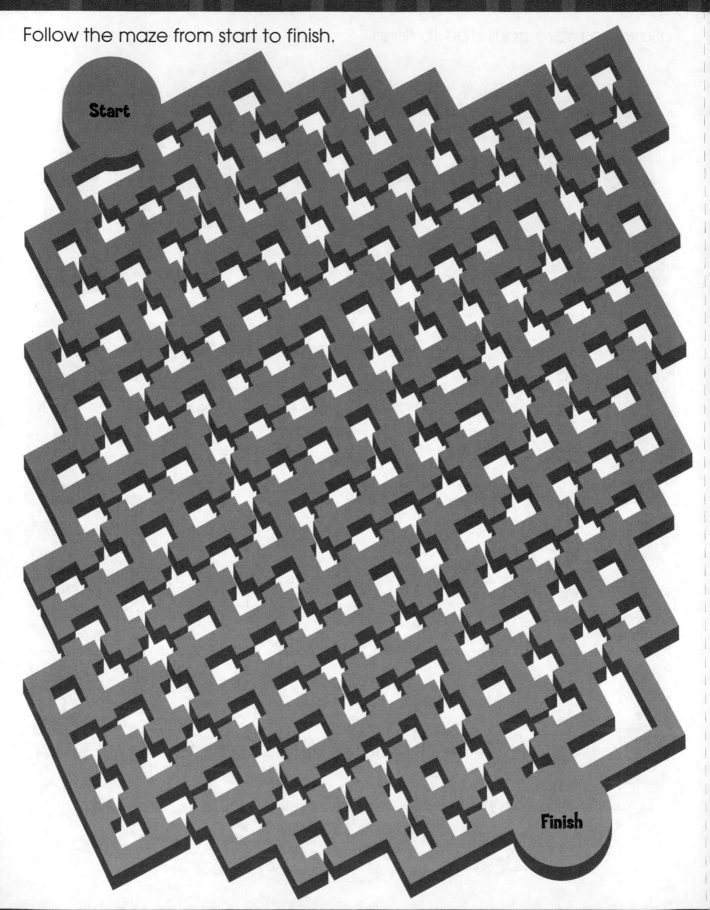

Mazes

EAT RIGHT!

Help the mouse get to the snack.

Start

Finish

Mazes

DON'T BE SO CRABBY!

Help the crab get to the shell.

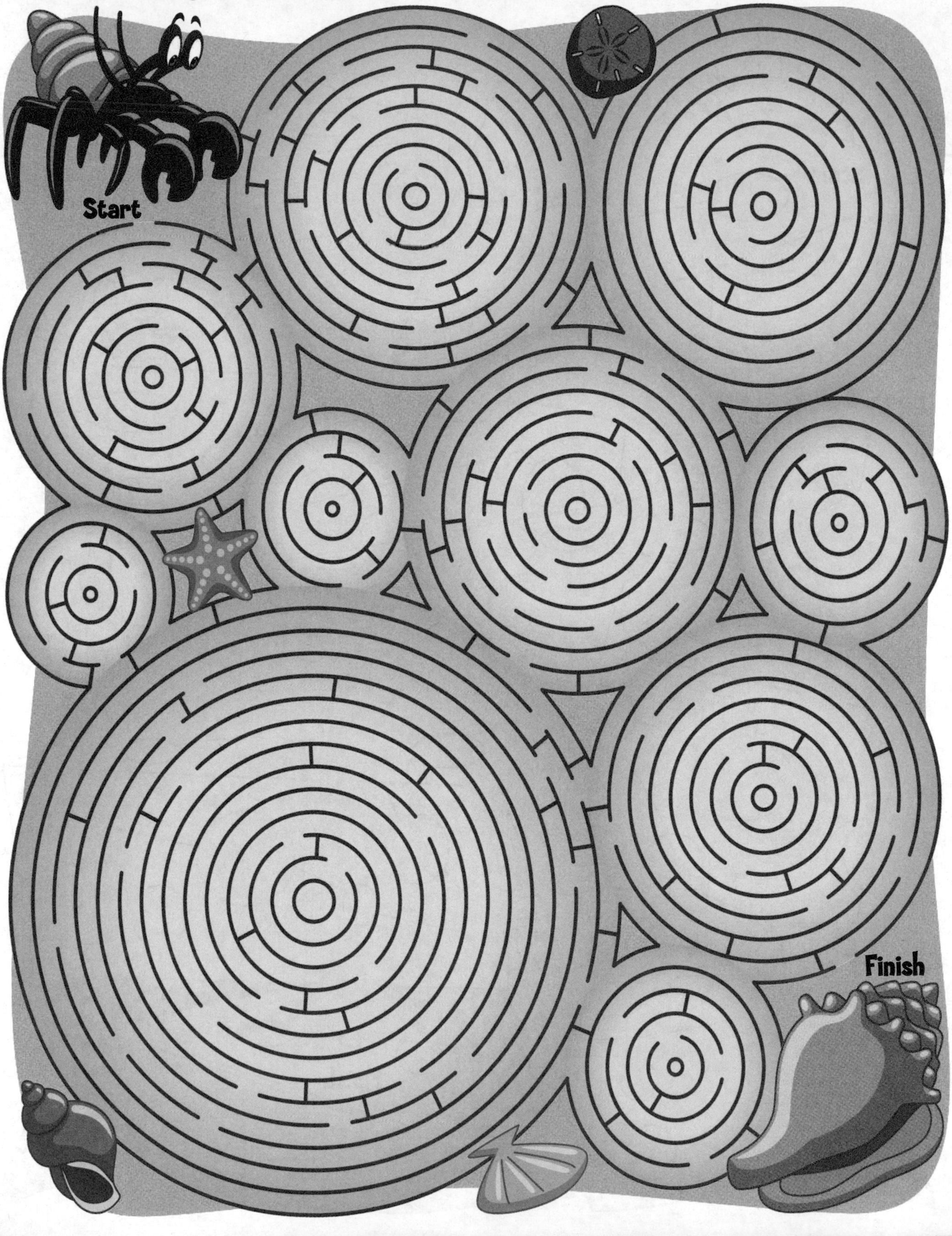

Start

Finish

RUN FROM THE MUMMY!

Help the man escape the mummy.

Start

Finish

Mazes

CROOKED

Follow the maze from start to finish.

Start

Finish

Mazes

IT'S STICKY!

Follow the maze from start to finish.

Start

Finish

Mazes

STAR GAZING

Follow the maze from start to finish.

Start

Finish

BROKEN BRICK WALL

Follow the maze from start to finish.

Start

Finish

©School Zone Publishing Company 06328

Mazes

Follow the maze from start to finish.

Start

Finish

Help the monkey find her way through the leaves.

Mazes

DON'T STEP IN THE LAVA

Follow the maze from start to finish.

GREEN GOO!

Follow the maze from start to finish.

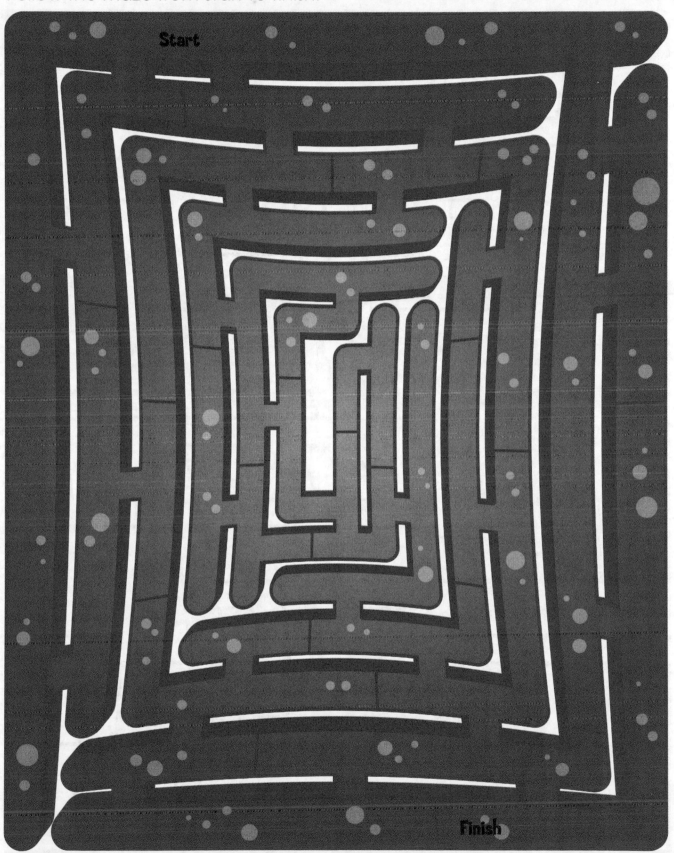

Start

Finish

Mazes

LABYRINTH OF COLOR

Follow the maze from start to finish.

Start

Finish

Mazes

CHOPPING WOOD

Follow the maze from start to finish.

Start

Finish

Mazes

HOT, HOT, HOT!

Follow the maze from start to finish.

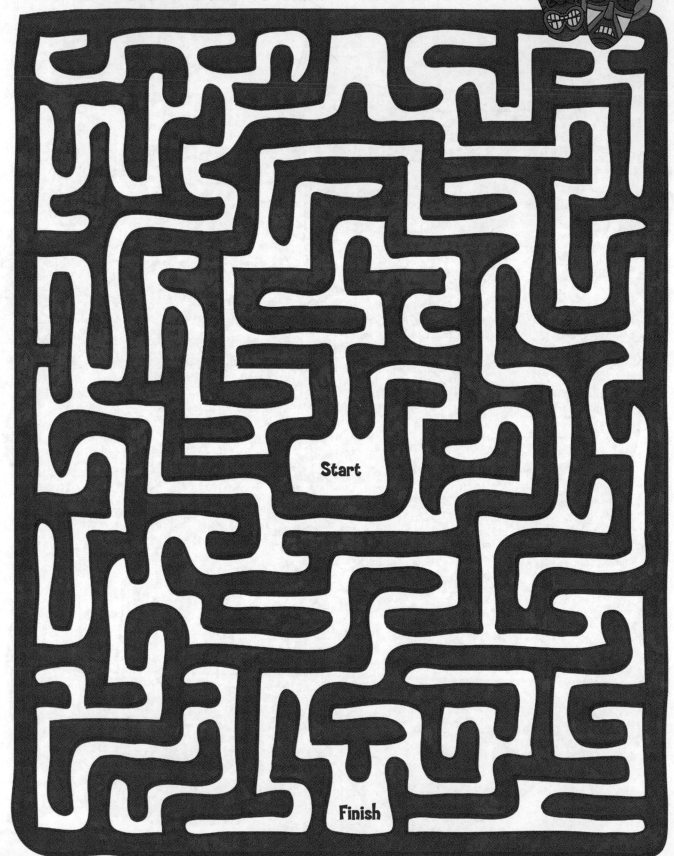

Start

Finish

COLORFUL CONFUSION

Follow the maze from start to finish.

Mazes

Follow the maze from start to finish.

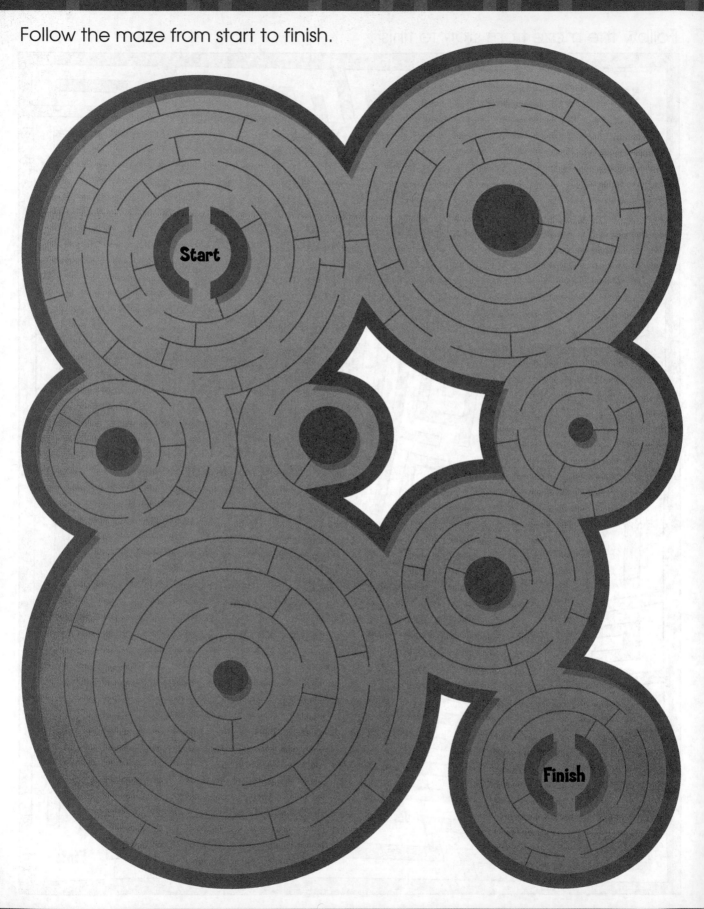

GOLDEN PATH

Follow the maze from start to finish.

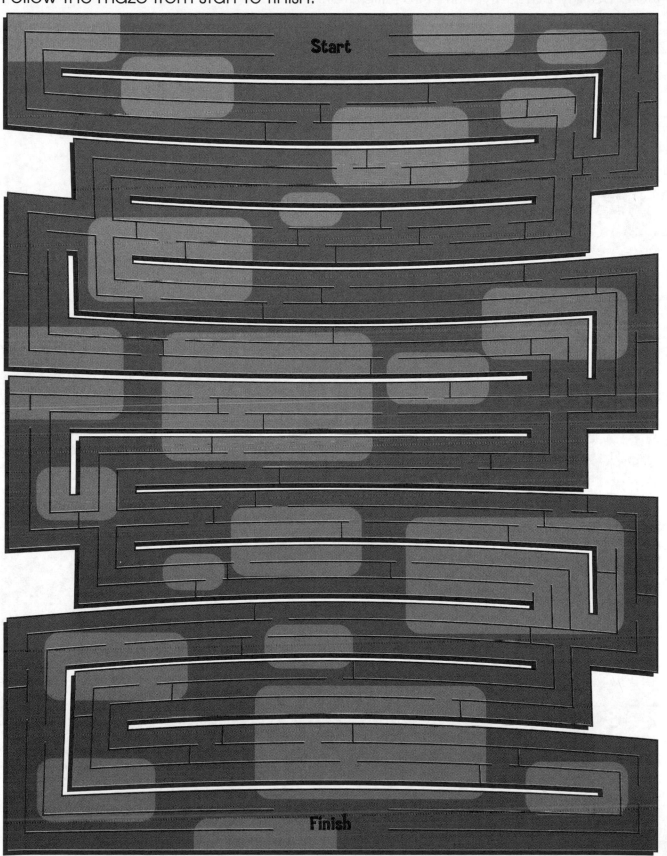

Mazes

BUTTERFLY'S BUDDY

Help Benny Butterfly visit Allie Alligator.

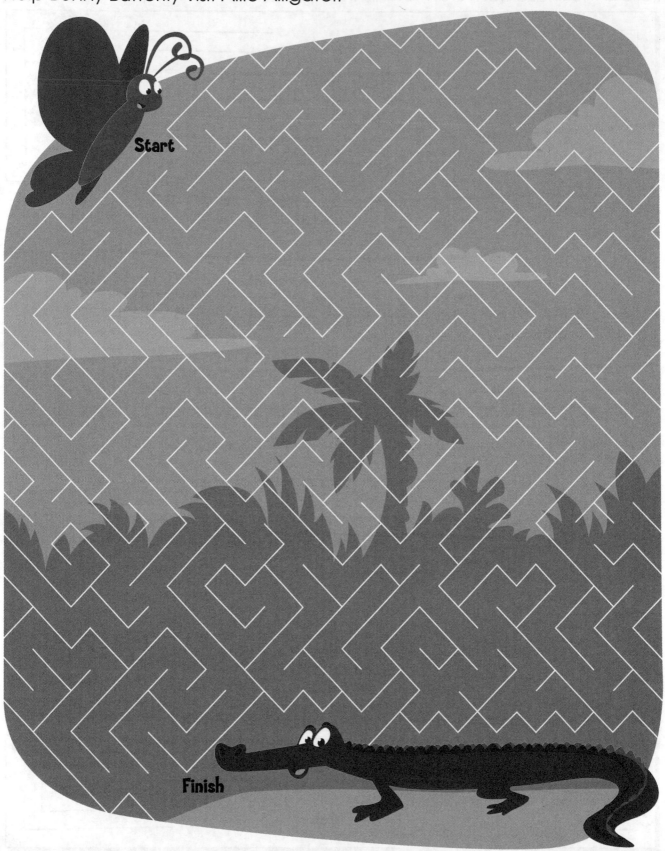

Start

Finish

BEYOND THE CITY

Follow the maze from start to finish.

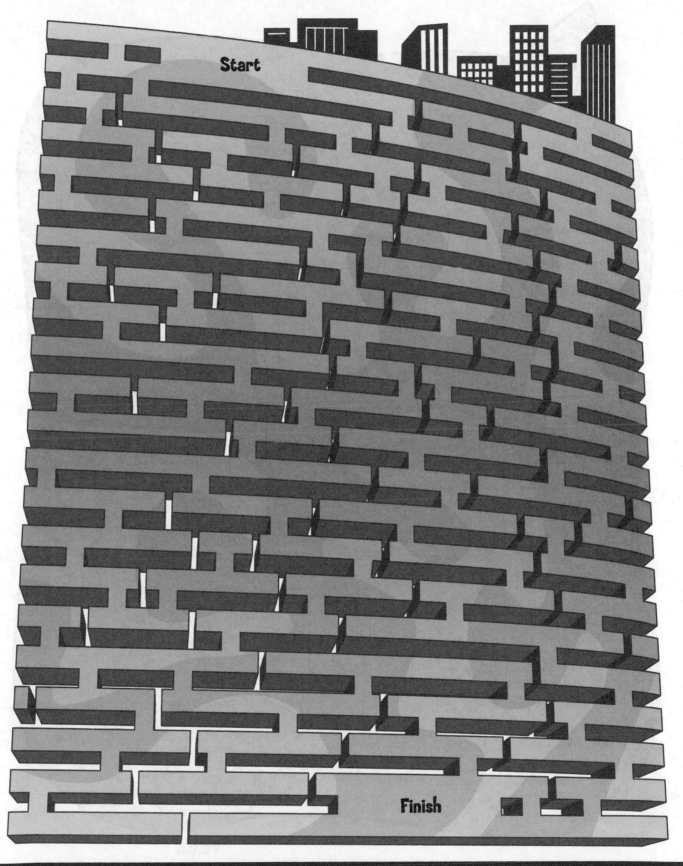

Start

Finish

Mazes

Help the squid swim through the water.

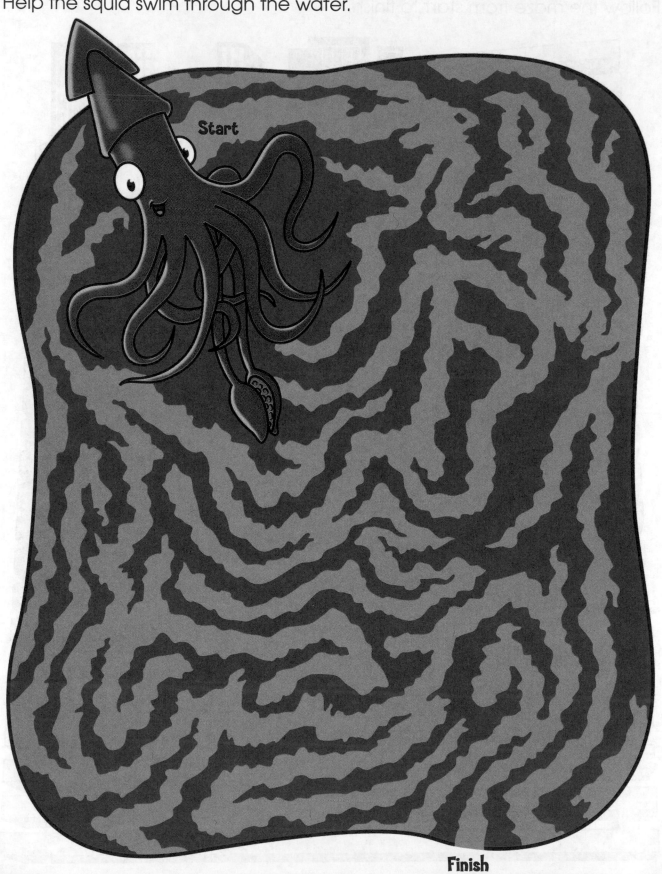

Start

Finish

Follow the maze from start to finish.

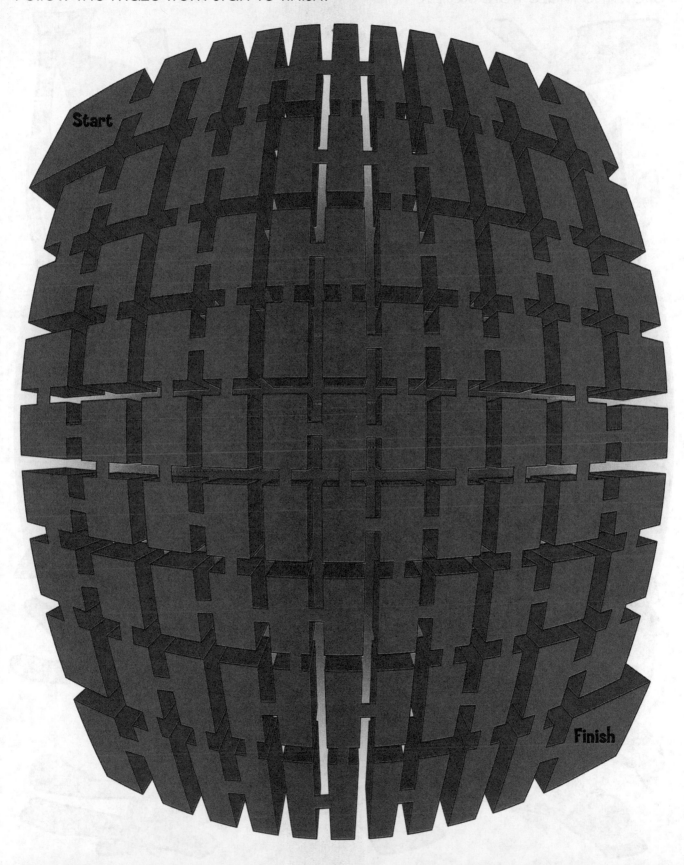

Mazes

CRAWLING WITH BUGS

Follow the maze from start to finish.

Start

Finish

Help the goldfish find the treasure.

Mazes

INTERSECTIONS

Follow the maze from start to finish.

Mazes

AROUND WE GO!

Follow the maze from start to finish.

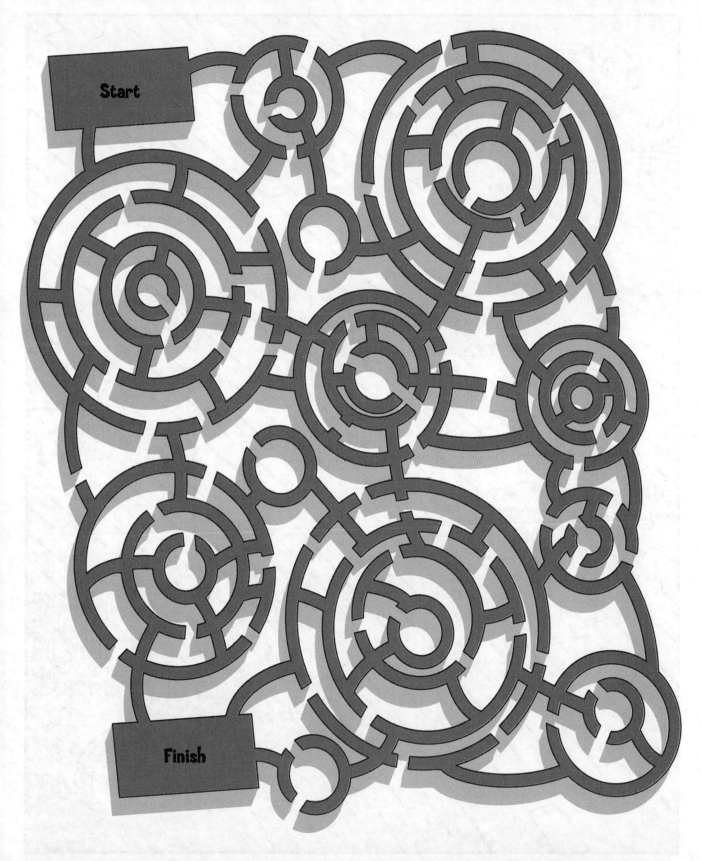

Start

Finish

Mazes

FORGOTTEN NUT

Help the chipmunk find the acorn.

Start

Finish

Mazes   ©School Zone Publishing Company 06328

WEAVE IN AQUA

Follow the maze from start to finish.

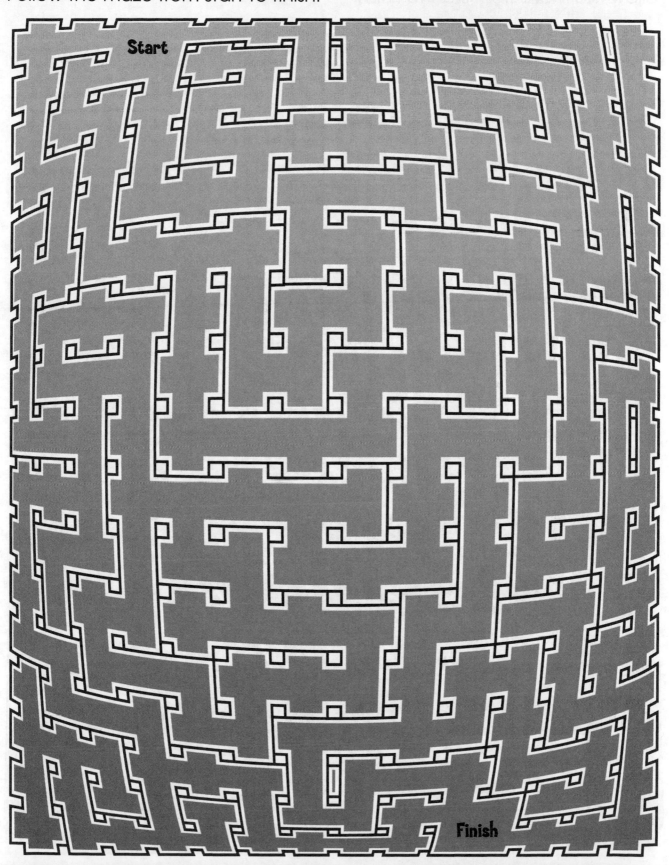

©School Zone Publishing Company 06328

Mazes

BASEMENT BLUES

Follow the maze from start to finish.

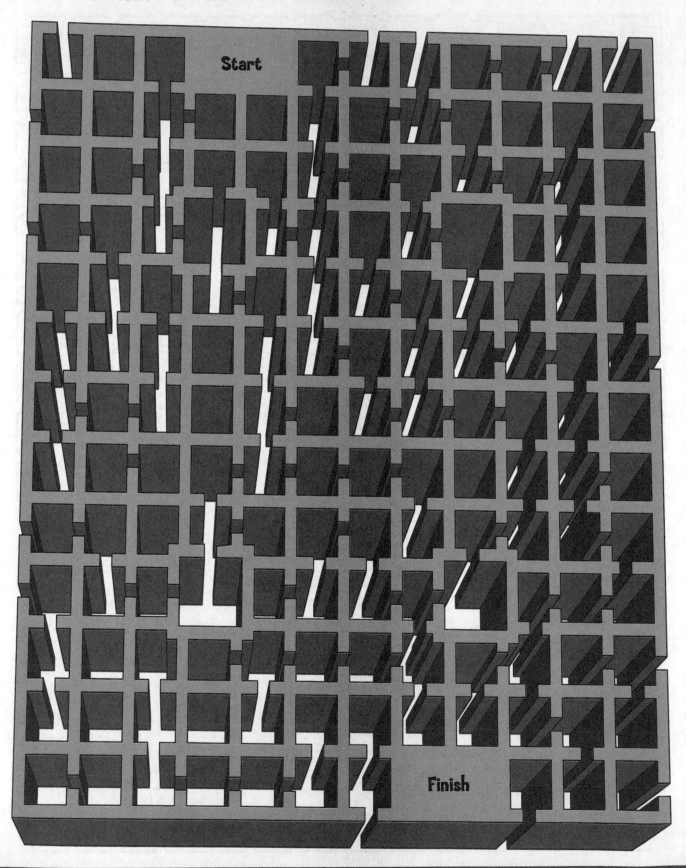

Help the skateboarder get to the bottom of the ramp.

Start

Finish

Mazes

Follow the maze from start to finish.

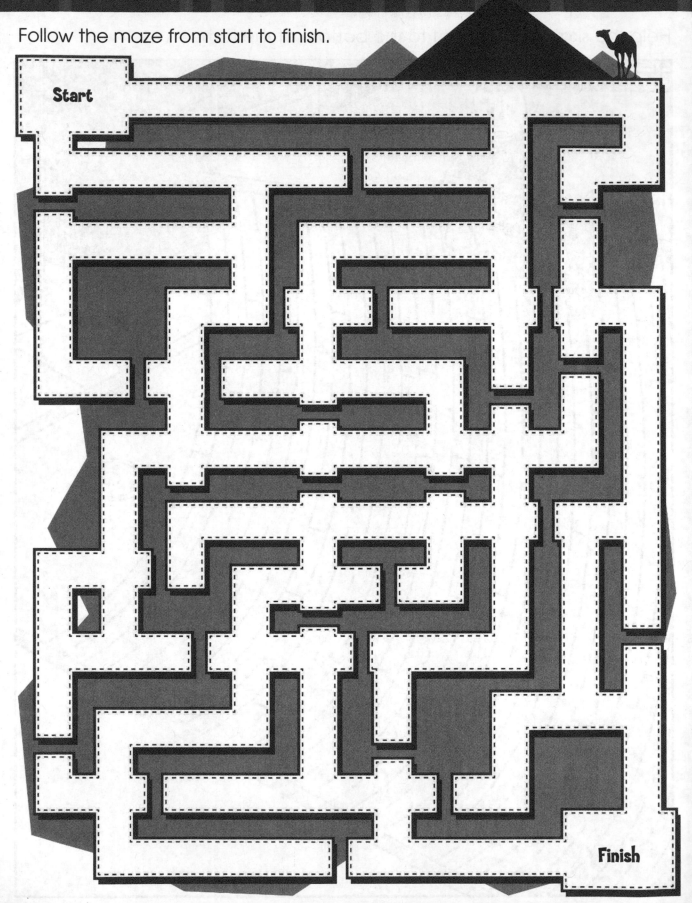

Start

Finish

©School Zone Publishing Company 06328

SQUARE DANCE

Follow the maze from start to finish.

Start

Finish

Mazes

ORANGE POWER!

Follow the maze from start to finish.

Follow the maze from start to finish.

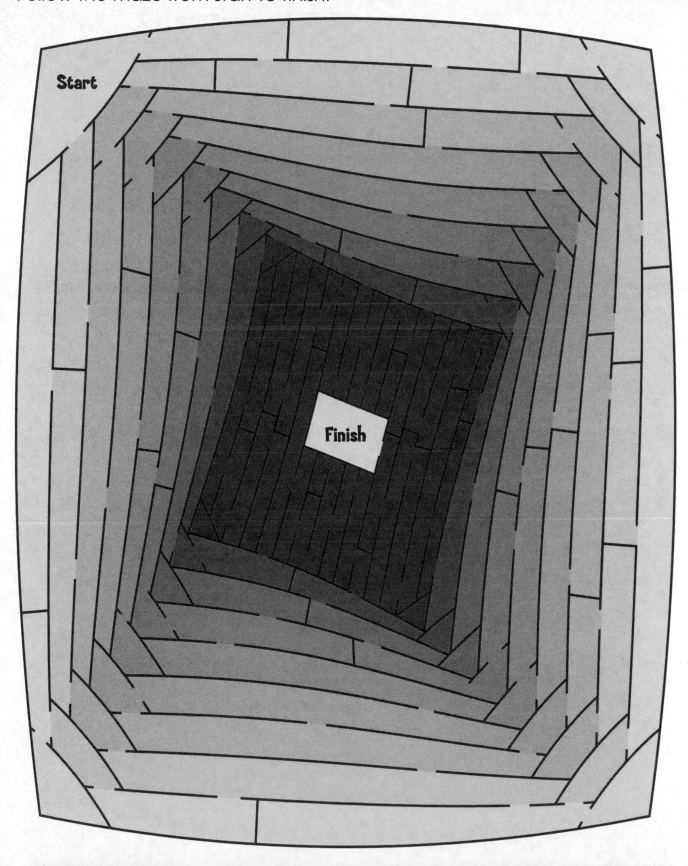

Start

Finish

Mazes

ORANGE GROOVE

Follow the maze from start to finish.

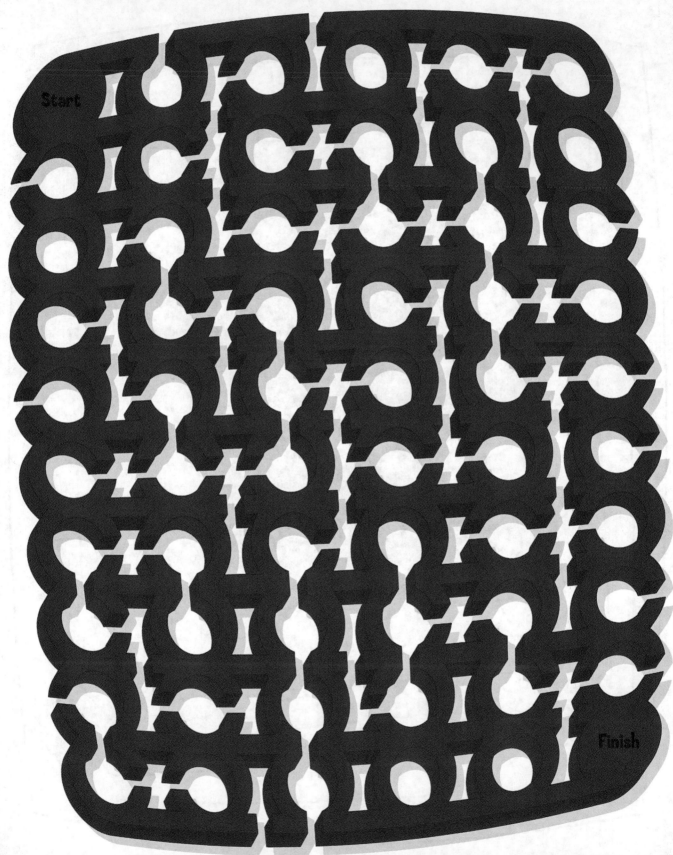

Start

Finish

Mazes   ©School Zone Publishing Company 06328

CENTER GLOW

Follow the maze from start to finish.

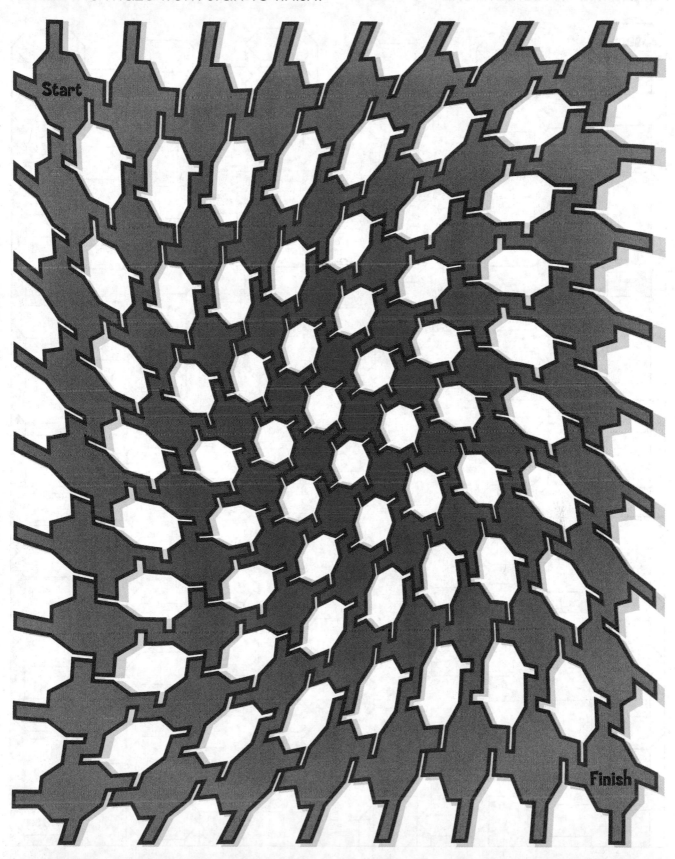

Mazes

STEP DOWN

Follow the maze from start to finish.

Start

Finish

HONEYCOMB

Follow the maze from start to finish.

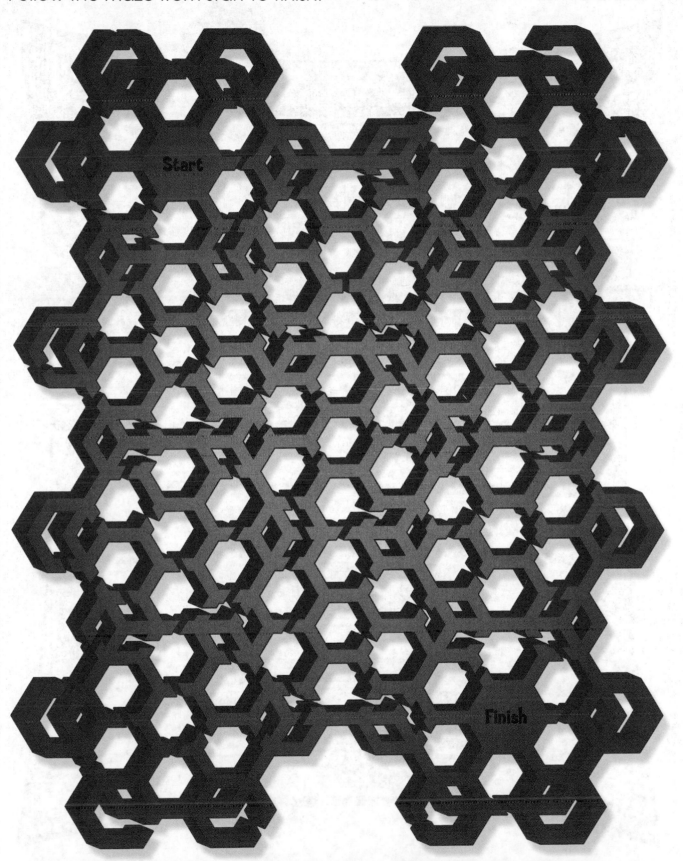

Start

Finish

Mazes

SUNNY DAY

Follow the maze from start to finish.

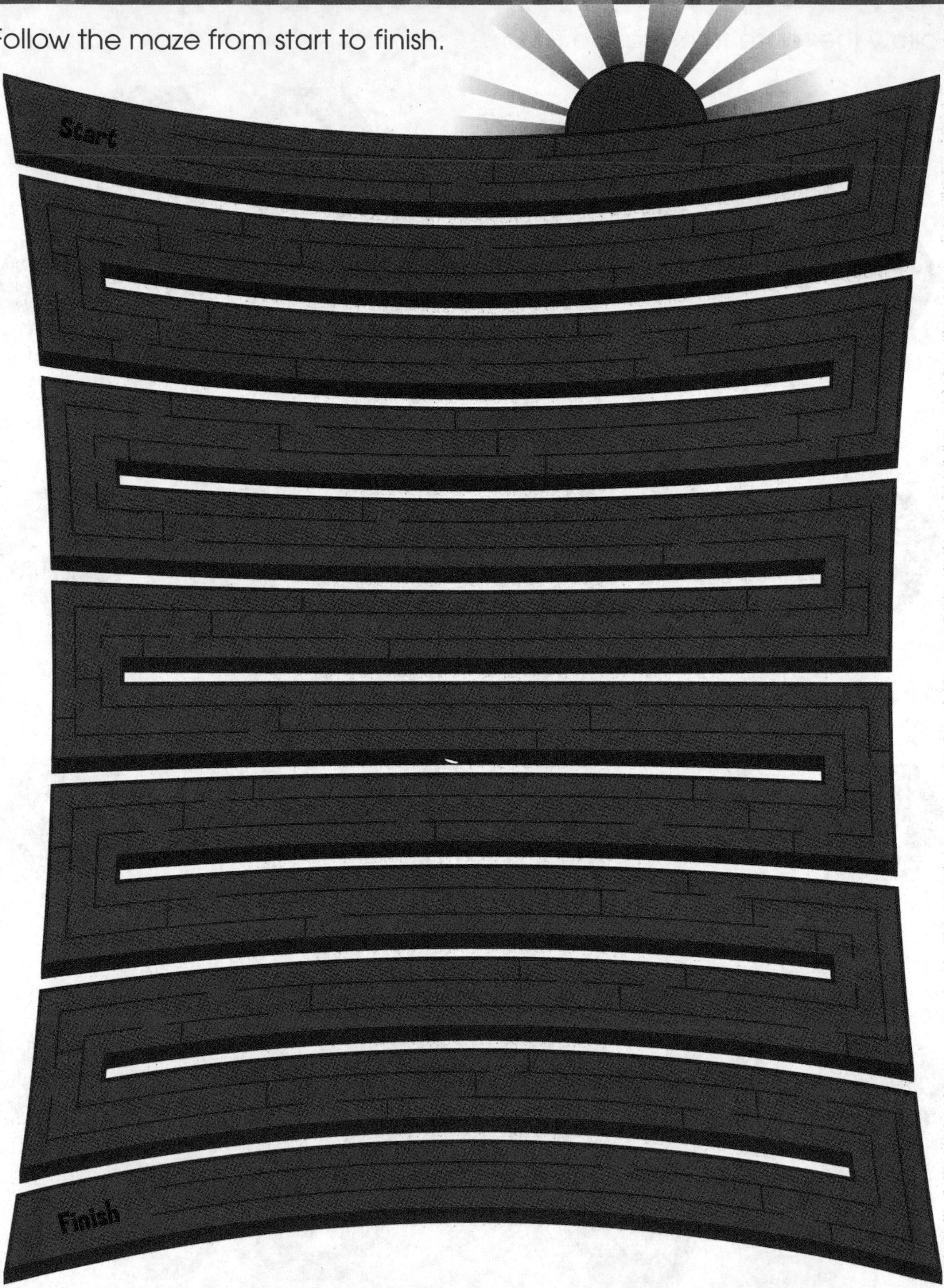

Start

Finish

GOT THE BLUES

Follow the maze from start to finish.

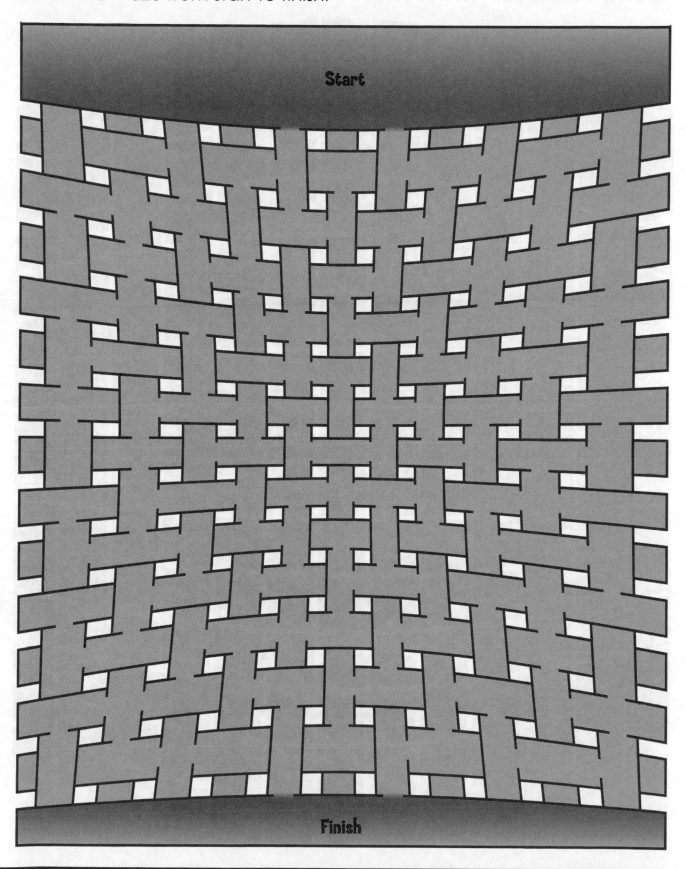

Start

Finish

Mazes

Follow the maze from start to finish.

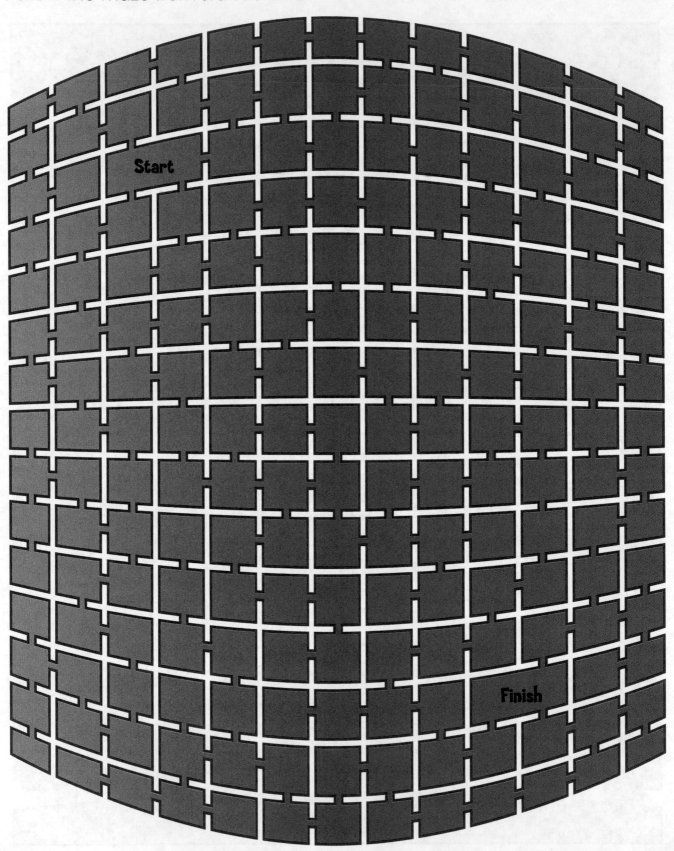

SEARCHING FOR SEASHELLS

Follow the maze from start to finish.

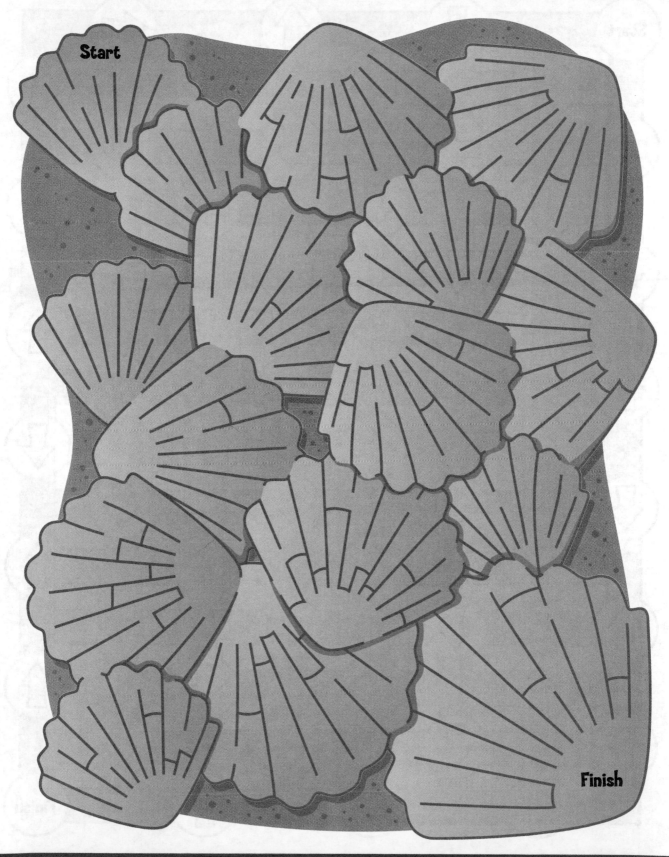

Start

Finish

Mazes

FOLLOWING DIRECTIONS

Follow the arrows through the maze to get from start to finish.

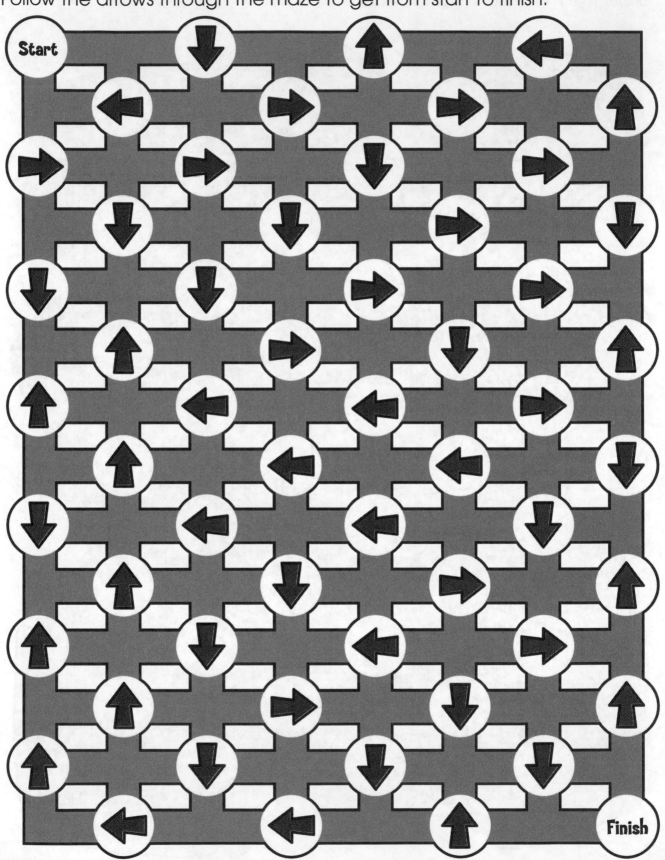

Mazes

COOL CUBE

Follow the maze from start to finish.

Mazes

ANSWER KEY

Note: Only one solution is shown for each maze, but other paths are possible.

Page 1

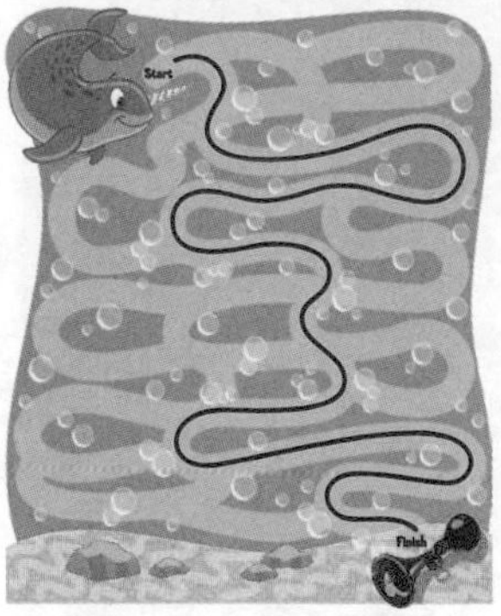

Page 2

Page 3

Page 4

Page 5

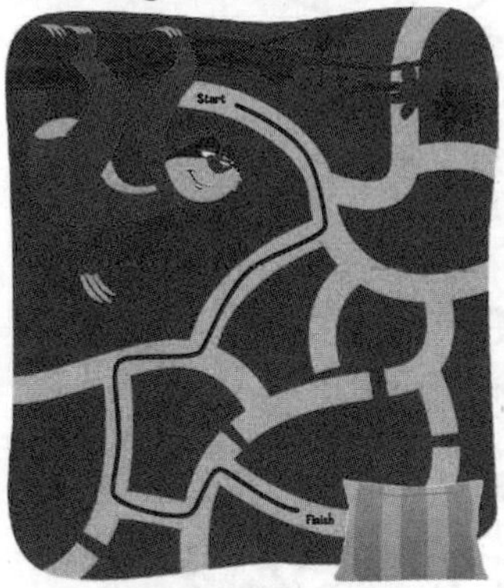

Page 6

Page 7

Page 8

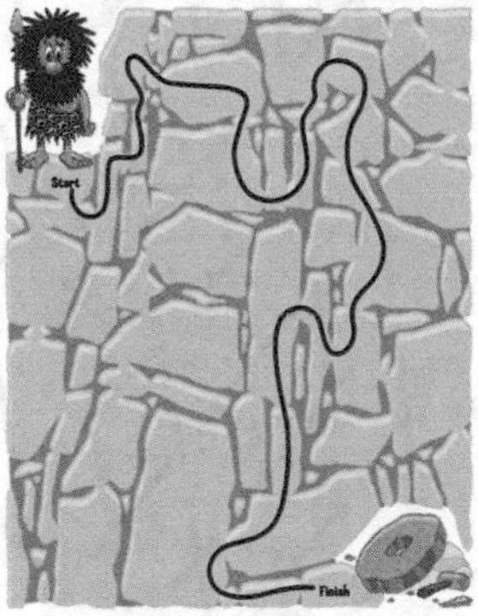

Page 9

Page 10

Page 11

Page 12

Page 13

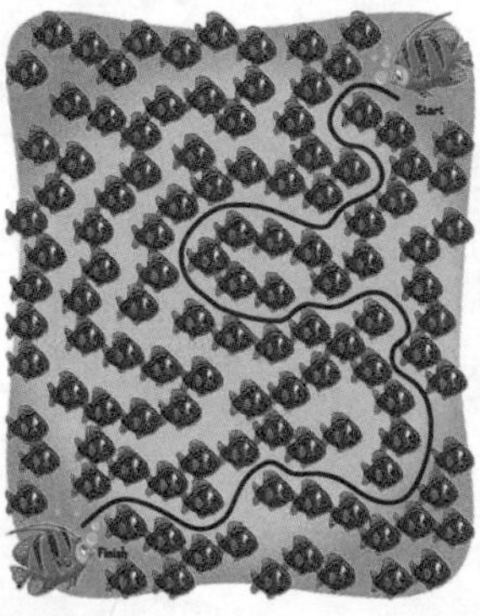

Page 14

Page 15

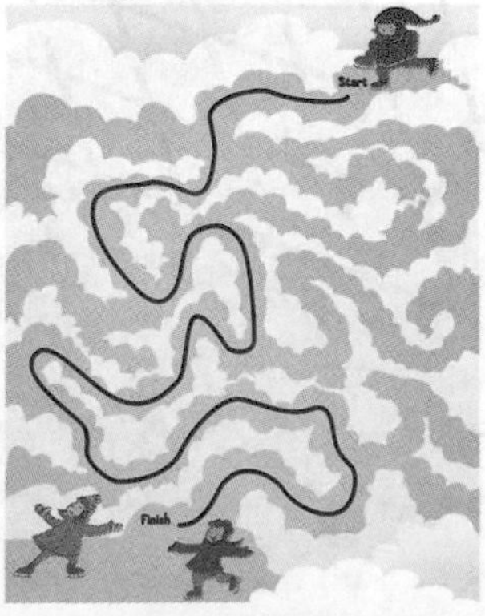

Page 16

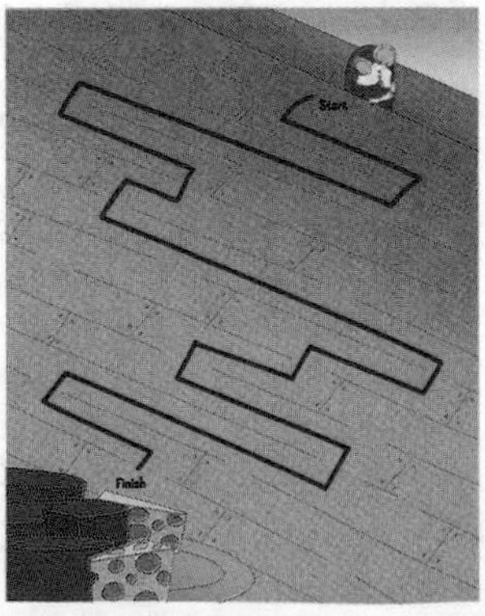

302

ANSWER KEY

Note: Only one solution is shown for each maze, but other paths are possible.

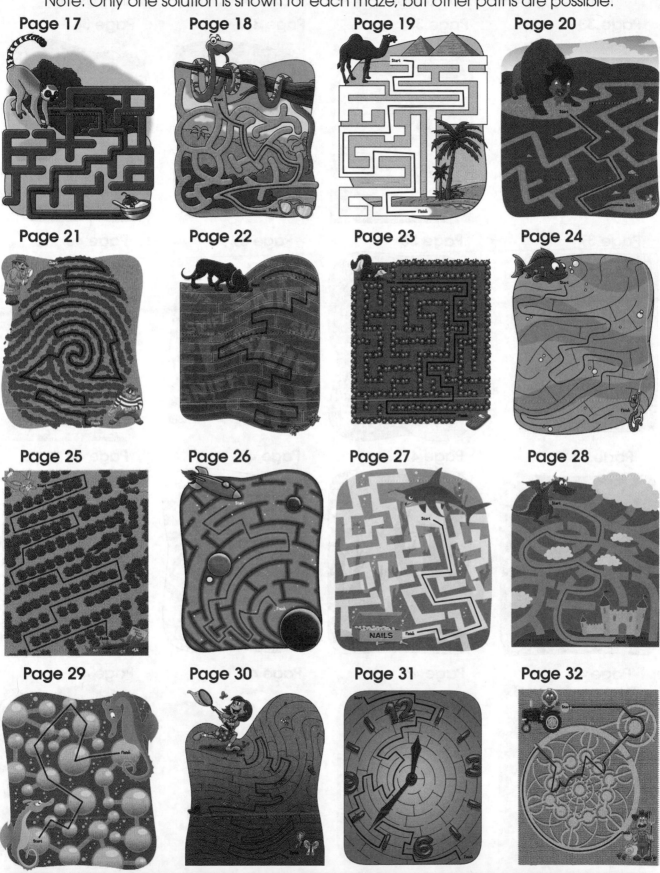

©School Zone Publishing Company 06328

Answer Key

ANSWER KEY

Note: Only one solution is shown for each maze, but other paths are possible.

Page 33

Page 34

Page 35

Page 36

Page 37

Page 38

Page 39

Page 40

Page 41

Page 42

Page 43

Page 44

Page 45

Page 46

Page 47

Page 48

ANSWER KEY

Note: Only one solution is shown for each maze, but other paths are possible.

Page 49

Page 50

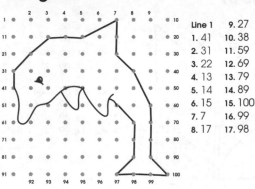

Line 1	9. 27	18. 97
1. 41	10. 38	19. 88
2. 31	11. 59	20. 78
3. 22	12. 69	21. 68
4. 13	13. 79	22. 57
5. 14	14. 89	
6. 15	15. 100	
7. 7	16. 99	
8. 17	17. 98	

Page 51

Page 52

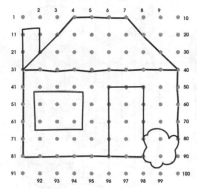

Line 1	9. 36	18. 71	Line 2
1. 80	10. 35	19. 81	1. 40
2. 70	11. 34	20. 82	2. 29
3. 60	12. 33	21. 83	3. 18
4. 50	13. 32	22. 84	4. 7
5. 40	14. 31	23. 85	5. 6
6. 39	15. 41	24. 86	6. 5
7. 38	16. 51	25. 87	7. 4
8. 37	17. 61	26. 88	8. 13

Page 53

Page 54

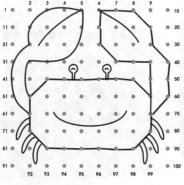

Line 1	9. 62	18. 69	27. 16
1. 59	10. 72	19. 60	28. 26
2. 48	11. 83	20. 50	29. 37
3. 47	12. 84	21. 40	30. 38
4. 46	13. 85	22. 29	31. 39
5. 45	14. 86	23. 19	32. 49
6. 44	15. 87	24. 8	33. 59
7. 43	16. 88	25. 7	
8. 52	17. 79	26. 6	

Page 55

Page 56

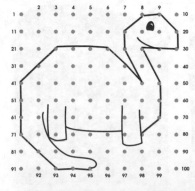

Line 1			
1. 78	8. 20	15. 26	22. 61
2. 69	9. 9	16. 25	23. 71
3. 59	10. 8	17. 24	24. 82
4. 49	11. 17	18. 23	25. 93
5. 28	12. 27	19. 32	26. 94
6. 29	13. 48	20. 41	27. 95
7. 30	14. 37	21. 51	

Page 57

305

Answer Key

Note: Only one solution is shown for each maze, but other paths are possible.

Page 58

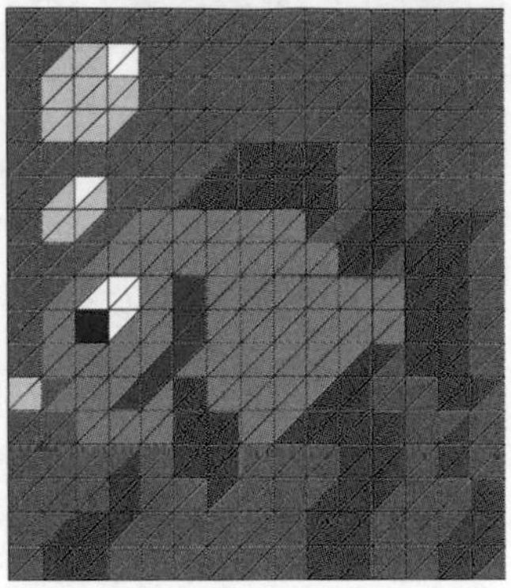

Page 59

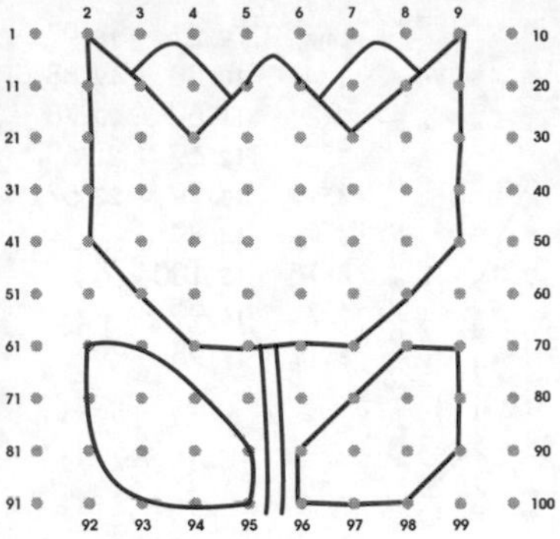

Line 1
1. 15
2. 24
3. 13
4. 2
5. 12
6. 22
7. 32
8. 42
9. 53
10. 64
11. 65
12. 66
13. 67
14. 58
15. 49
16. 39
17. 29
18. 19
19. 9
20. 18
21. 27
22. 16

Line 2
1. 69
2. 68
3. 77
4. 86
5. 96
6. 97
7. 98
8. 89
9. 79
10. 69

Page 60

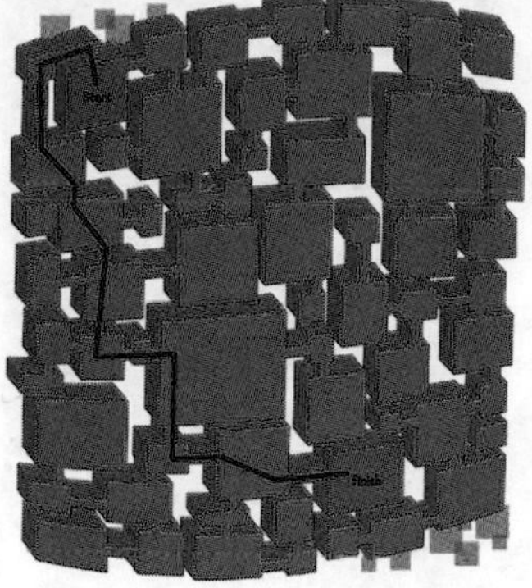

Page 61

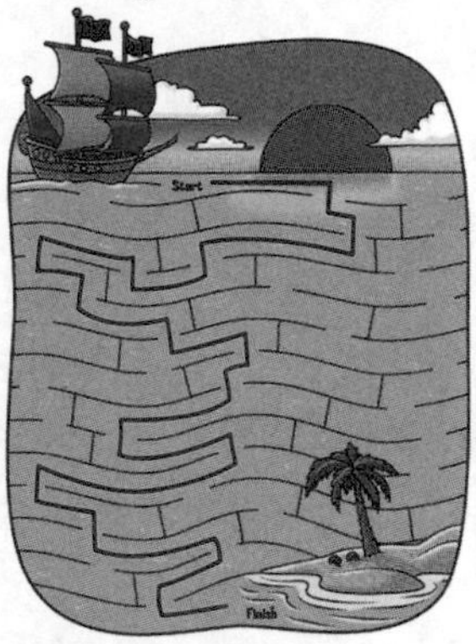

Page 62

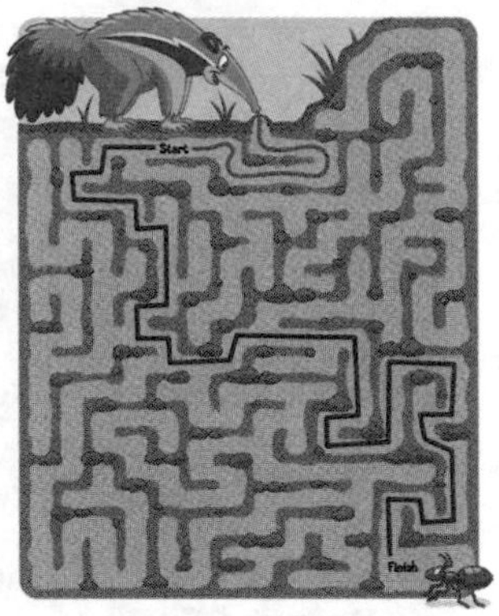

Page 63

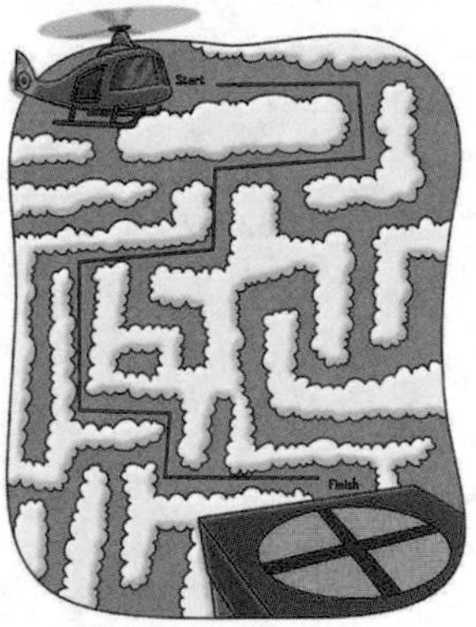

Page 64

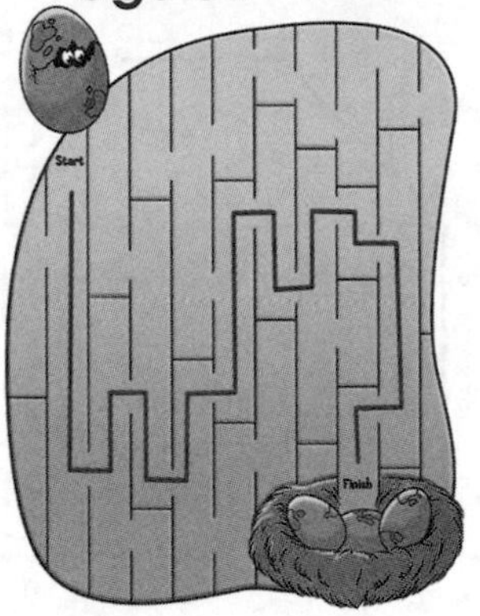

Page 65

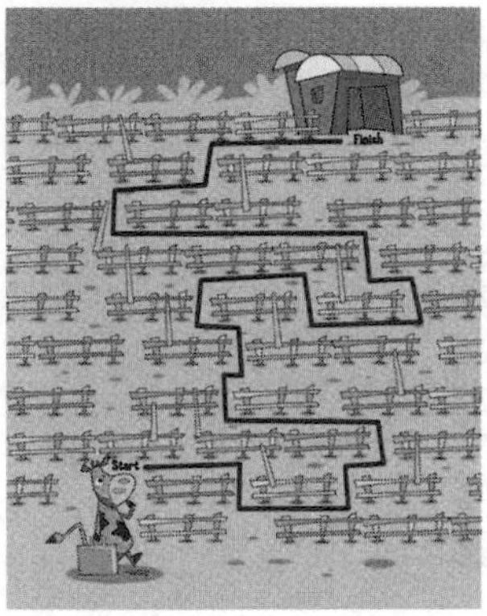

Page 66

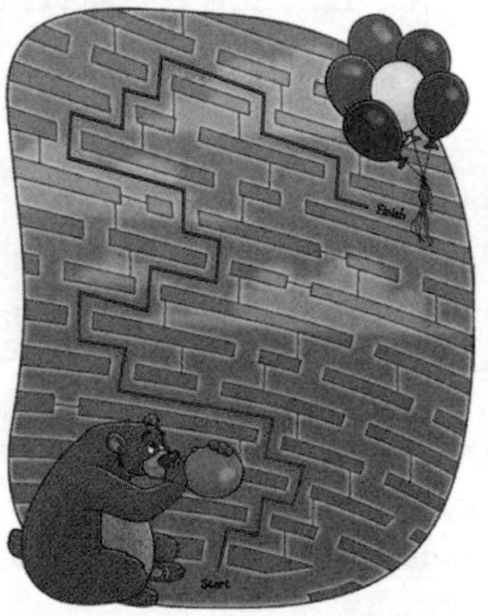

Page 67

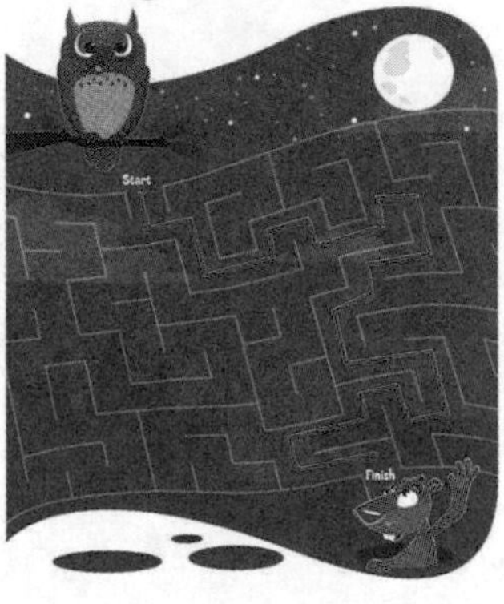

Page 68

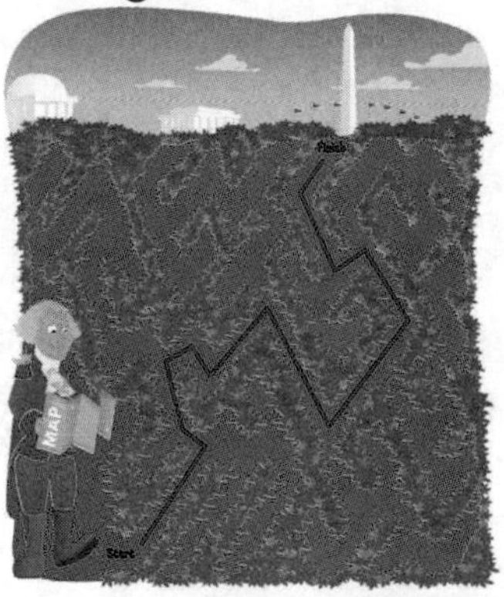

Page 69

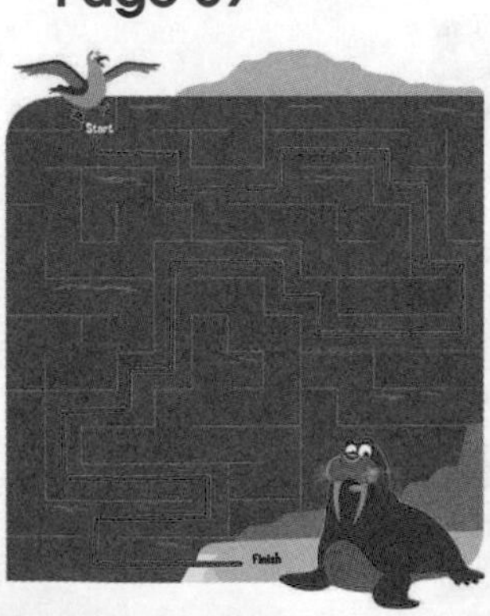

Page 70

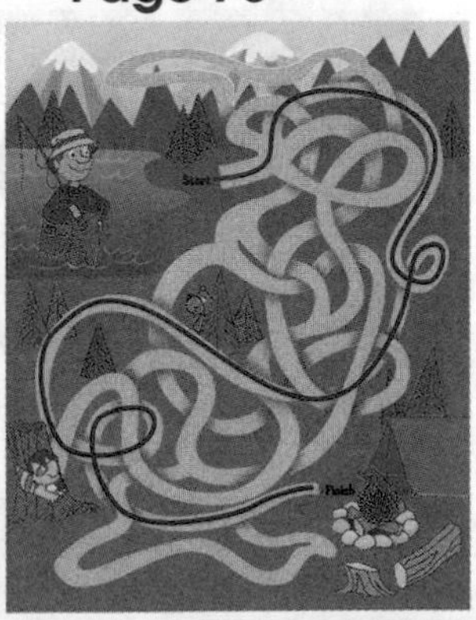

Page 71

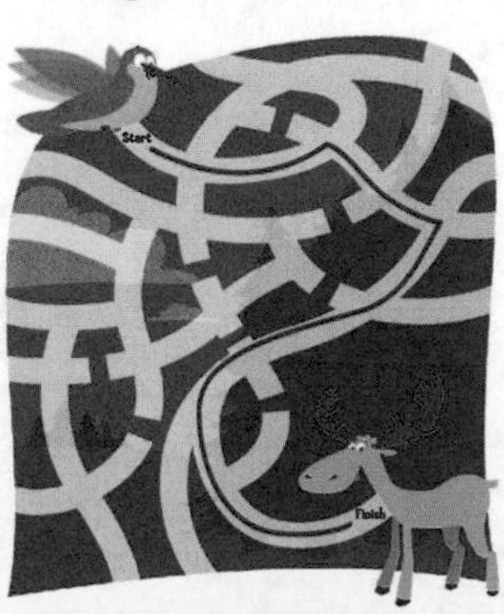

Page 72

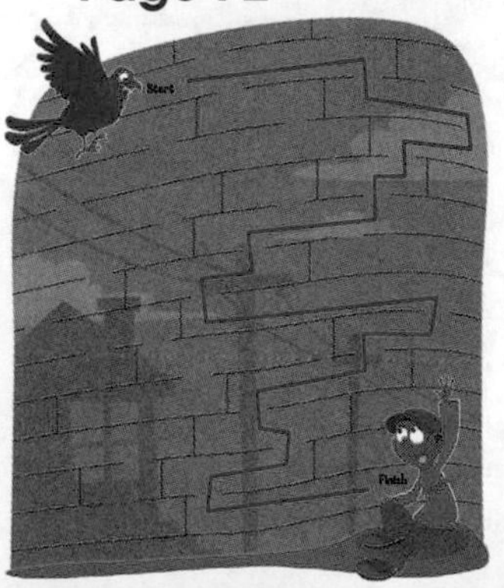

©School Zone Publishing Company 06328

ANSWER KEY

Note: Only one solution is shown for each maze, but other paths are possible.

Page 73 **Page 74** **Page 75** **Page 76**

Page 77 **Page 78** **Page 79** **Page 80**

Page 81 **Page 82** **Page 83** **Page 84**

Page 85 **Page 86** **Page 87** **Page 88**

©School Zone Publishing Company 06328

Answer Key

ANSWER KEY

Note: Only one solution is shown for each maze, but other paths are possible.

Page 89

Page 90
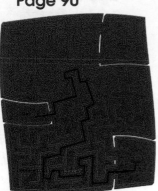

Page 91

Page 92

Page 93

Page 94

Page 95
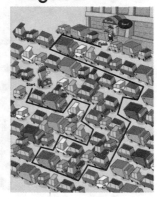

Page 96

Page 97

Page 98

Page 99
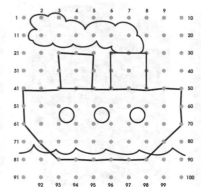

Line 1	8. 25	16. 61	24. 79
1. 50	9. 24	17. 72	25. 70
2. 49	10. 23	18. 83	26. 60
3. 48	11. 33	19. 84	27. 50
4. 47	12. 43	20. 85	
5. 46	13. 42	21. 86	
6. 45	14. 41	22. 87	
7. 35	15. 51	23. 88	

Page 100
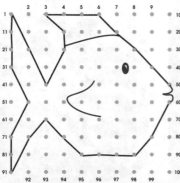

Page 101
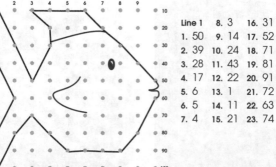

Line 1	8. 3	16. 31	24. 85
1. 50	9. 14	17. 52	25. 86
2. 39	10. 24	18. 71	26. 87
3. 28	11. 43	19. 81	27. 88
4. 17	12. 22	20. 91	28. 79
5. 6	13. 1	21. 72	29. 60
6. 5	14. 11	22. 63	
7. 4	15. 21	23. 74	

Page 102
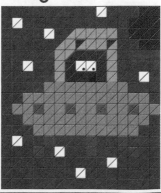

ANSWER KEY

Note: Only one solution is shown for each maze, but other paths are possible.

Page 103

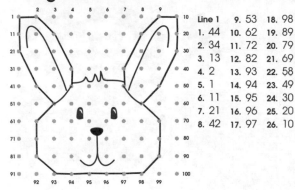

Line 1	9. 53	18. 98	27. 9
1. 44	10. 62	19. 89	28. 18
2. 34	11. 72	20. 79	29. 37
3. 13	12. 82	21. 69	30. 47
4. 2	13. 93	22. 58	
5. 1	14. 94	23. 49	
6. 11	15. 95	24. 30	
7. 21	16. 96	25. 20	
8. 42	17. 97	26. 10	

Page 104

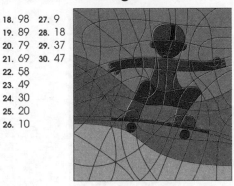

Page 105

Line 1	9. 83	18. 49	Line 2
1. 4	10. 94	19. 38	1. 44
2. 13	11. 95	20. 28	2. 54
3. 23	12. 96	21. 18	3. 45
4. 33	13. 97	22. 7	4. 55
5. 42	14. 88	23. 6	5. 46
6. 52	15. 79	24. 5	6. 57
7. 62	16. 69	25. 4	7. 47
8. 72	17. 59		

Page 106

Page 107

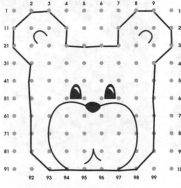

Line 1	9. 20	18. 3	27. 82
1. 98	10. 9	19. 2	28. 93
2. 89	11. 8	20. 11	29. 94
3. 79	12. 17	21. 21	30. 95
4. 69	13. 27	22. 32	31. 96
5. 59	14. 26	23. 42	32. 97
6. 49	15. 25	24. 52	33. 98
7. 39	16. 24	25. 62	
8. 30	17. 14	26. 72	

Page 108

Page 109

Page 110

Page 111

Page 112

Page 113

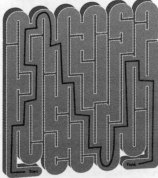

309

Answer Key

ANSWER KEY

Note: Only one solution is shown for each maze, but other paths are possible.

Page 114

Page 115

Page 116

Page 117

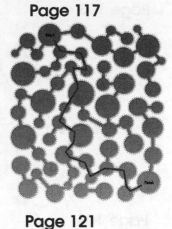

Page 118

Page 119

Page 120

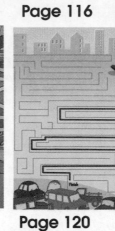

Page 121

Page 122

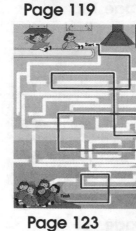

Page 123

Page 124

Page 125

Page 126

Page 127

Page 128

Page 129

ANSWER KEY

Note: Only one solution is shown for each maze, but other paths are possible.

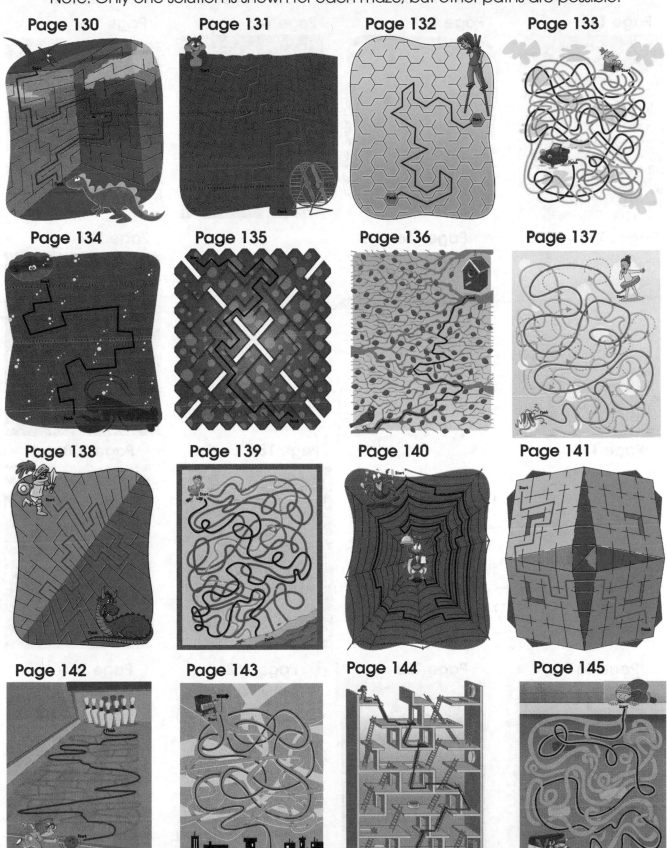

Page 130

Page 131

Page 132

Page 133

Page 134

Page 135

Page 136

Page 137

Page 138

Page 139

Page 140

Page 141

Page 142

Page 143

Page 144

Page 145

Answer Key

ANSWER KEY

Note: Only one solution is shown for each maze, but other paths are possible.

Page 146

Page 147

Page 148

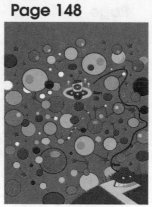

Page 149

Pages 150 – 155

Solutions will vary.

Page 156

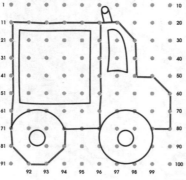

	Line 1		9. 28	Line 2		9. 41
	1. 76	10. 38		1. 74	10. 31	
	2. 66	11. 48		2. 84	11. 21	
	3. 56	12. 49		3. 93	12. 11	
	4. 46	13. 60		4. 92	13. 12	
	5. 36	14. 70		5. 81	14. 13	
	6. 26	15. 80		6. 71	15. 14	
	7. 16	16. 79		7. 61	16. 15	
	8. 17			8. 51	17. 16	

Page 157

Page 158

Line 1		9. 63	18. 49	5. 76
1. 16	10. 64		19. 38	6. 75
2. 15	11. 65		20. 27	7. 74
3. 24	12. 66		21. 16	8. 73
4. 33	13. 67		Line 2	9. 72
5. 42	14. 68		1. 80	10. 71
6. 51	15. 69		2. 79	
7. 61	16. 70		3. 78	
8. 62	17. 60		4. 77	

Page 159

Page 160

Page 161

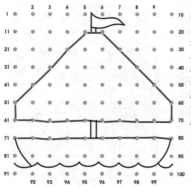

Page 162

Page 163

Page 164

Answer Key

ANSWER KEY

Note: Only one solution is shown for each maze, but other paths are possible.

Page 165

Page 166

Page 167

Page 168

Page 169

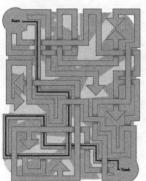

Page 170

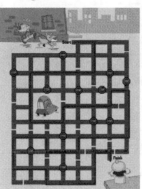

Page 171

Page 172

Page 173

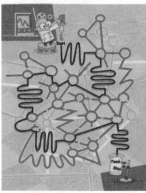

Page 174

Page 175

Page 176

Page 177

Page 178

Page 179

Page 180

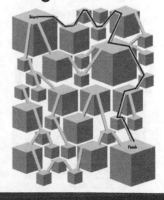

313

©School Zone Publishing Company 06328

ANSWER KEY

Note: Only one solution is shown for each maze, but other paths are possible.

Page 181

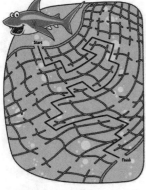

Page 182

Page 183

Page 184

Page 185

Page 186

Page 187

Page 188

Page 189

Page 190

Page 191

Page 192

Page 193

Page 194

Page 195

Page 196

314

ANSWER KEY

Note: Only one solution is shown for each maze, but other paths are possible.

Page 197

Page 198

Page 199

Page 200

Pages 201 – 210

Solutions will vary.

Page 211
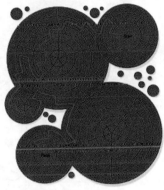

Page 212
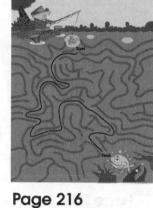

Page 213

Page 214

Page 215

Page 216
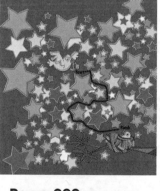

Page 217

Page 218

Page 219

Page 220

Page 221

315

Note: Only one solution is shown for each maze, but other paths are possible.

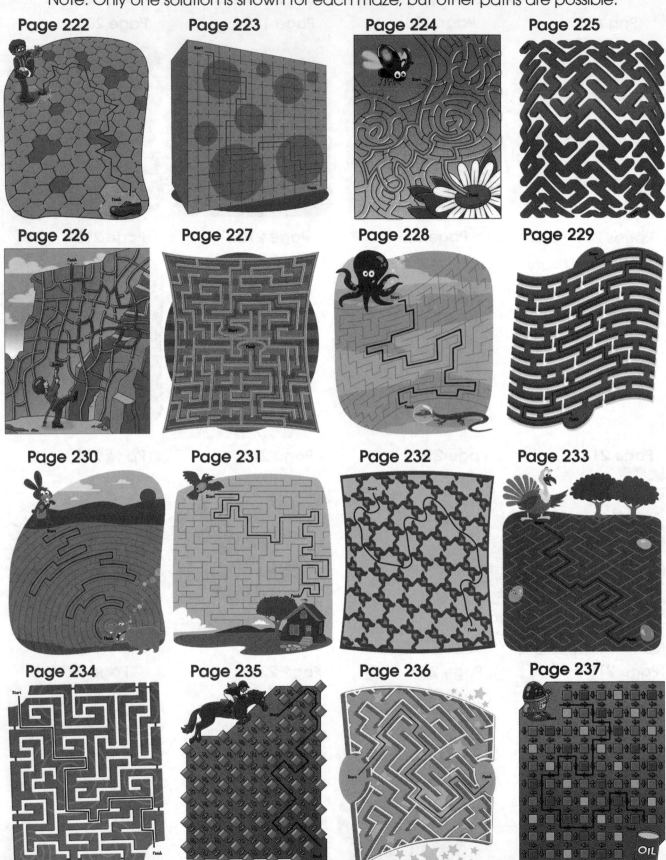

Page 222

Page 223

Page 224

Page 225

Page 226

Page 227

Page 228

Page 229

Page 230

Page 231

Page 232

Page 233

Page 234

Page 235

Page 236

Page 237

ANSWER KEY

Note: Only one solution is shown for each maze, but other paths are possible.

Page 238

Page 239

Page 240

Page 241

Page 242

Page 243

Page 244

Page 245

Page 246

Page 247

Page 248

Page 249

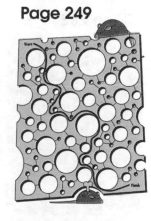

Page 250

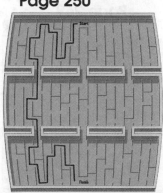

Page 251

Page 252

Page 253

©School Zone Publishing Company 06328

Page 254

Page 255

Page 256

Page 257

Page 258

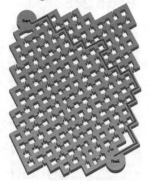

Page 259

Page 260

Page 261

Page 262

Page 263

Page 264

Page 265

Page 266

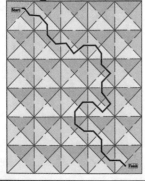

Page 267

Page 268

Page 269

ANSWER KEY

Note: Only one solution is shown for each maze, but other paths are possible.

Page 270

Page 271

Page 272

Page 273

Page 274

Page 275

Page 276

Page 277

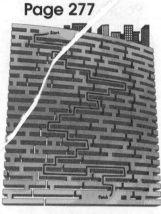

Page 278

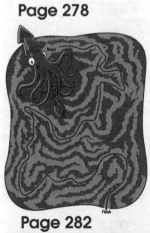

Page 279

Page 280

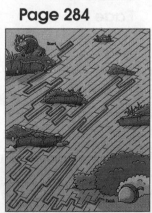

Page 281

Page 282

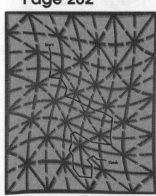

Page 283

Page 284

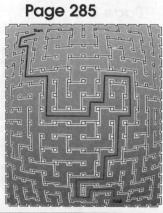

Page 285

ANSWER KEY

Note: Only one solution is shown for each maze, but other paths are possible.

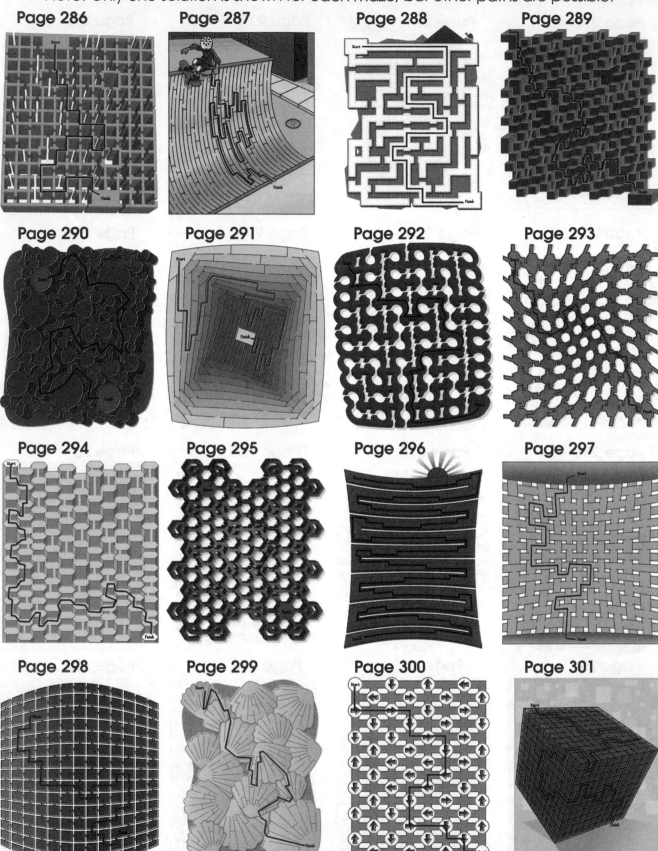

Page 286   Page 287   Page 288   Page 289

Page 290   Page 291   Page 292   Page 293

Page 294   Page 295   Page 296   Page 297

Page 298   Page 299   Page 300   Page 301

320

Big Puzzle Play Mazes & More 06328